LLC

Beginner's Guide

A

Dummies Guide Book on How to Start Your Own Business

Table of Contents

INTRODUCTION 5

PURPOSE OF THE BOOK 5
WHO SHOULD READ THIS BOOK? 6
HOW TO USE THIS BOOK 6

CHAPTER 1: UNDERSTANDING LLCS 8

1.1   WHAT IS AN LLC? 8
1.2   ADVANTAGES OF AN LLC 11
1.3   DISADVANTAGES OF AN LLC 14
1.4   LLC VS. OTHER BUSINESS STRUCTURES 18

CHAPTER 2: PLANNING YOUR LLC 23

2.1 IS AN LLC RIGHT FOR YOU? 23
2.2 DEFINING YOUR BUSINESS GOALS 27
2.3 NAMING YOUR LLC 32
2.4 CHOOSING A REGISTERED AGENT 37
2.5 LLC OPERATING AGREEMENT 42

CHAPTER 3: FORMATION OF AN LLC 48

3.1 STEPS TO FORMING AN LLC 48
3.2 STATE-SPECIFIC REQUIREMENTS 54
3.3 FILING ARTICLES OF ORGANIZATION 59
3.4 LLC FORMATION COSTS 63

CHAPTER 4: MANAGING YOUR LLC 68

4.1 LLC OPERATING AGREEMENT DETAILS 68
4.2 MANAGING MEMBERS AND MANAGERS 73
4.3 ROLES AND RESPONSIBILITIES 79
4.4 RECORD KEEPING AND COMPLIANCE 84

CHAPTER 5: TAXES AND FINANCES 90

5.1 UNDERSTANDING LLC TAXES 90
5.2 TAX OPTIONS FOR LLCS 95
5.3 FINANCIAL RECORD KEEPING 101
5.4 BUDGETING AND FINANCIAL PLANNING 106

CHAPTER 6: LEGAL REQUIREMENTS AND COMPLIANCE 111

6.1 FEDERAL AND STATE LAWS 111
6.2 ANNUAL REPORTS AND FEES 114
6.3 MAINTAINING GOOD STANDING 118
6.4 DEALING WITH LEGAL ISSUES 122

CHAPTER 7: GROWING YOUR LLC 127

7.1 BUSINESS DEVELOPMENT STRATEGIES 127
7.2 MARKETING AND SALES 132
7.3 SCALING YOUR OPERATIONS 137
7.4 HIRING EMPLOYEES AND CONTRACTORS 142

CHAPTER 8: PROTECTING YOUR LLC 148

8.1 LIABILITY PROTECTION 148
8.2 INTELLECTUAL PROPERTY 152
8.3 INSURANCE FOR YOUR LLC 156
8.4 RISK MANAGEMENT 160

CHAPTER 9: CHANGES AND DISSOLUTION 165

9.1 AMENDING YOUR LLC 165
9.2 ADDING OR REMOVING MEMBERS 168
9.3 DISSOLVING YOUR LLC 172
9.4 HANDLING DEBTS AND OBLIGATIONS 176

CHAPTER 10: RESOURCES AND TOOLS 180

10.1 USEFUL WEBSITES AND ONLINE RESOURCES 180
10.2 RECOMMENDED BOOKS AND COURSES 184
10.3 PROFESSIONAL SERVICES: WHEN TO SEEK HELP 186
10.4 TEMPLATES AND CHECKLISTS 191

APPENDICES 195

A.   GLOSSARY OF TERMS 195
B. SAMPLE LLC OPERATING AGREEMENT 195
B.   STATE-BY-STATE LLC RESOURCES 196
C.   FREQUENTLY ASKED QUESTIONS (FAQ) 197
RECAP OF KEY POINTS 199
ENCOURAGEMENT AND NEXT STEPS 199

Introduction

S tarting your own business is an exciting journey filled with opportunities and challenges. Whether you're a first-time entrepreneur or an experienced business owner looking to restructure, this guide is designed to help you navigate the process of forming and managing a Limited Liability Company (LLC).

Purpose of the Book

The purpose of this book is to provide a comprehensive, step-by-step guide to creating and running a successful LLC. We aim to demystify the complexities of business formation and management, offering clear, practical advice that you can apply immediately. From understanding what an LLC is to handling taxes, compliance, and growth, this book covers all the essential aspects you need to know.

Who Should Read This Book?

This guide is perfect for:

Aspiring Entrepreneurs: If you're considering starting your own business and want to explore the LLC structure, this book will give you a solid foundation.

Small Business Owners: If you already own a business and are thinking about restructuring it as an LLC, you'll find valuable insights and detailed instructions here.

Freelancers and Consultants: If you want to formalize your business operations and gain legal protection, forming an LLC might be the right choice for you.

Anyone Interested in Business: Even if you're not ready to start your own LLC, understanding this business structure can be beneficial for your future endeavors.

How to Use This Book

This guide is organized to take you from the basics to more advanced topics in a logical sequence. Here's how you can get the most out of it:

Start at the Beginning: If you're new to LLCs, we recommend reading from the beginning to understand the fundamental concepts and benefits.

Skip Around as Needed: If you're already familiar with the basics, feel free to jump to specific chapters that address your current needs or questions.

Use the Checklists and Templates: Throughout the book, you'll find practical tools like checklists and templates designed to help you implement the advice provided.

Refer Back Often: Keep this book handy as a reference guide. The business landscape can change, and revisiting certain sections can provide valuable reminders and updates.

Embarking on Your LLC Journey

The journey of forming and managing an LLC is filled with learning experiences and growth opportunities. By choosing to educate yourself and prepare thoroughly, you are setting a solid foundation for your business success. This guide is here to support you every step of the way, making the process as straightforward and manageable as possible.

So, let's get started. Turn the page and dive into the world of LLCs, where your entrepreneurial dreams can become a reality. Welcome to the LLC Guide, and here's to your business success!

Chapter 1: Understanding LLCs

1.1 What is an LLC?

S tarting a business involves making several critical decisions, and choosing the right business structure is among the most important. One popular option is the Limited Liability Company, commonly known as an LLC. But what exactly is an LLC, and why might it be the right choice for your business?

An LLC, or Limited Liability Company, is a hybrid business structure that combines the limited liability protection of a corporation with the flexibility and tax benefits of a partnership or sole proprietorship. This unique combination makes LLCs an attractive option for many entrepreneurs and small business owners.

Key Characteristics of an LLC

Limited Liability Protection: One of the main advantages of an LLC is that it provides limited liability protection to its owners, known as members. This means that the personal assets of the members (such as homes, cars, and personal bank accounts) are typically protected from business debts and claims. In other words, if the LLC faces a lawsuit or incurs debt, the members' personal assets are not usually at risk.

Flexible Management Structure: LLCs offer flexibility in management. They can be managed by the members (member-managed) or by appointed managers (manager-managed). This flexibility allows businesses to tailor the management structure to suit their needs and preferences.

Pass-Through Taxation: Unlike corporations, which are subject to double taxation (once at the corporate level and again at the shareholder level), LLCs benefit from pass-through taxation. This means that the business income is reported on the personal tax returns of the members, avoiding the need to pay corporate taxes. This can result in significant tax savings for LLC members.

Ease of Formation and Maintenance: Forming an LLC is generally easier and involves less paperwork than forming a corporation. The ongoing maintenance requirements, such as annual reports and record-keeping, are also typically simpler and less burdensome.

Why Choose an LLC?

The LLC structure is designed to offer the best of both worlds: the protection and credibility of a corporation and the operational flexibility and tax benefits of a partnership or sole proprietorship. Here are some scenarios where an LLC might be the right choice:

Small Businesses and Startups: LLCs are ideal for small businesses and startups that want to protect their personal assets while enjoying flexible management and tax options.

Professional Services: Many professionals, such as consultants, freelancers, and real estate agents, choose LLCs to formalize their business operations and limit their liability.

Family-Owned Businesses: Family-owned and closely-held businesses often benefit from the simple structure and operational flexibility of an LLC.

Joint Ventures: When two or more parties come together for a joint venture, an LLC can provide a clear framework for management and profit-sharing while protecting individual members' assets.

Conclusion

Understanding what an LLC is and its key characteristics is the first step in deciding whether this business structure is right for you. LLCs offer a unique blend of liability protection, tax advantages, and management flexibility, making them a popular choice for a wide range of businesses. In the next sections, we'll dive deeper into the advantages and disadvantages of LLCs, helping you make an informed decision about your business's future.

By grasping the fundamentals of what an LLC is, you're on your way to making a knowledgeable decision that could significantly impact your business's success and growth.

1.2 Advantages of an LLC

Choosing the right business structure is crucial for any entrepreneur. The Limited Liability Company (LLC) is a popular choice, and for good reasons. It offers numerous advantages that can make running a business smoother and more secure. Let's explore the key benefits of forming an LLC.

1. Limited Liability Protection

One of the most compelling reasons to choose an LLC is the limited liability protection it provides. This means that the personal assets of the LLC's owners, known as members, are generally protected from the company's debts and legal obligations. If the business incurs debt or is sued, members' personal assets, such as their homes and personal savings, are typically not at risk. This protection allows entrepreneurs to take business risks without jeopardizing their personal financial security.

2. Pass-Through Taxation

LLCs benefit from a tax structure known as pass-through taxation. Unlike corporations, which can be subject to double taxation (where income is taxed at both the corporate and personal levels), an LLC's income is only taxed once. The business's profits and losses pass through to the members, who report them on their individual tax returns. This can simplify the tax process and potentially result in significant tax savings.

3. Flexible Management Structure

LLCs offer a flexible management structure. Members can choose to manage the LLC themselves (member-managed) or appoint managers to run the business (manager-managed). This flexibility allows businesses to create a management system that best suits their needs. For instance, a small business with few members might opt for a member-managed structure, while a larger business might prefer a manager-managed approach to streamline operations.

4. Minimal Compliance Requirements

Compared to corporations, LLCs have fewer ongoing compliance requirements. While corporations must hold annual meetings, keep detailed records, and adhere to strict reporting guidelines, LLCs generally have simpler and less burdensome requirements. This ease of maintenance can save time and reduce administrative costs, allowing business owners to focus more on growing their business.

5. Enhanced Credibility

Forming an LLC can enhance your business's credibility. The LLC designation after your business name signals to clients, partners, and investors that your business is formally registered and operates with a level of professionalism and permanence.

This can help build trust and attract more business opportunities.

6. Flexible Profit Distribution

LLCs offer flexibility in how profits are distributed among members. Unlike corporations, which must distribute profits according to the number of shares owned, LLCs can distribute profits in any manner agreed upon by the members. This allows for more customized and equitable profit-sharing arrangements that reflect the contributions of each member.

7. Unlimited Membership

An LLC can have an unlimited number of members, which can be individuals, corporations, or even other LLCs. This flexibility makes it easier to bring in additional investors or partners, facilitating business growth and expansion. Furthermore, there are no restrictions on foreign ownership, allowing international members to participate in the LLC.

8. Versatile Uses

LLCs are versatile and can be used for various types of businesses, including:

Small businesses and startups: LLCs provide a straightforward structure for new ventures.

Real estate holdings: Investors often use LLCs to hold and manage real estate properties.

Professional services: Freelancers and consultants can benefit from the liability protection and tax advantages.

Family businesses: LLCs offer an organized way to manage family-owned enterprises.

The advantages of forming an LLC are substantial, making it an attractive option for many business owners. From limited liability protection and pass-through taxation to flexible management and profit distribution, LLCs offer a blend of benefits that can enhance both the operational and financial aspects of a business. Understanding these advantages is crucial in making an informed decision about whether an LLC is the right structure for your business.

In the next section, we will discuss the potential disadvantages of an LLC, ensuring you have a balanced view of this business structure before making your decision.

1.3 Disadvantages of an LLC

While the Limited Liability Company (LLC) offers numerous advantages, it is essential to consider its potential downsides as well. Understanding these disadvantages will help you make a well-informed decision about whether this business structure is the best fit for your needs. Here are some of the key drawbacks associated with forming an LLC.

1. Self-Employment Taxes

One of the primary financial disadvantages of an LLC, particularly for single-member LLCs, is the obligation to pay self-employment taxes. In a corporation, owners can be employees and receive a salary, which is subject to payroll taxes. In contrast, LLC members must pay self-employment taxes on their share of the profits, which can be higher than payroll taxes because they cover both the employer and employee portions of Social Security and Medicare taxes.

2. Cost of Formation and Maintenance

While forming an LLC is generally simpler and less expensive than forming a corporation, it still involves costs that can be significant, especially for small businesses. These costs include state filing fees, which can vary widely, and ongoing fees for annual reports or franchise taxes in some states. Additionally, if your LLC operates in multiple states, you may need to register and pay fees in each state, increasing your overall expenses.

3. Limited Life

In many states, an LLC has a limited lifespan. Unlike corporations, which can exist perpetually, an LLC may be required to dissolve upon the death, withdrawal, or bankruptcy of a member, unless otherwise stated in the operating agreement. This can create challenges for long-term planning and business continuity, making it essential to include provisions in the operating agreement to address these situations.

4. Complexity of Profit Distribution

While the flexibility of profit distribution can be an advantage, it can also lead to complexity and potential disputes among members. Unlike corporations, which have straightforward dividend distribution based on shares, LLCs can allocate profits and losses in any manner agreed upon by the members. This flexibility requires careful planning and clear documentation in the operating agreement to prevent misunderstandings and conflicts.

5. Less Prestige

In some industries, an LLC may not carry the same level of prestige as a corporation. Corporations are often perceived as larger, more established, and more professional entities, which can be advantageous when dealing with clients, investors, and partners. While an LLC can enhance credibility compared to a sole proprietorship or partnership, it may not always match the perceived status of a corporation.

6. Potential for Member Disputes

LLCs can face challenges related to member disputes, especially in multi-member LLCs. Differences in opinion regarding the management, profit distribution, and strategic direction of the business can lead to conflicts. It is crucial to have a well-drafted operating agreement that outlines the roles, responsibilities, and procedures for resolving disputes to mitigate this risk.

7. Limited Access to Capital

Raising capital can be more challenging for LLCs compared to corporations. While LLCs can bring in new members who contribute capital, they do not have the ability to issue stock, which is a primary method for corporations to raise funds. This limitation can make it harder for LLCs to attract large-scale investment, potentially restricting their growth opportunities.

8. Varying State Laws

LLCs are regulated at the state level, which means that the rules governing them can vary significantly from one state to another. This variability can create complexity for LLCs that operate in multiple states, requiring compliance with different regulations and potentially increasing administrative burdens. It is important to understand the specific requirements of each state where your LLC will do business.

While LLCs offer many attractive benefits, they also come with certain disadvantages that must be carefully considered. From self-employment taxes and formation costs to potential member disputes and limited access to capital, these drawbacks highlight the importance of thorough planning and consultation with legal and financial advisors. By understanding both the advantages and disadvantages, you can make an informed decision about whether an LLC is the right structure for your business.

1.4 LLC vs. Other Business Structures

Choosing the right business structure is a critical decision for any entrepreneur. Each structure offers distinct advantages and disadvantages that can significantly impact your business's operations, tax obligations, and legal protections. In this section, we will compare LLCs with other common business structures: sole proprietorships, partnerships, and corporations. This comparison will help you understand where an LLC stands in relation to these alternatives.

1. LLC vs. Sole Proprietorship

Sole Proprietorship: This is the simplest and most common form of business ownership, where a single individual owns and operates the business. There is no legal distinction between the owner and the business.

LLC Advantages Over Sole Proprietorship:

Limited Liability: Unlike a sole proprietorship, where the owner's personal assets are at risk, an LLC provides limited liability protection, shielding personal assets from business debts and legal actions.

Credibility: Forming an LLC can enhance the business's credibility with customers, suppliers, and potential investors, giving it a more professional appearance.

Tax Flexibility: An LLC offers more tax flexibility, allowing for pass-through taxation while providing options to be taxed as a sole proprietorship, partnership, S corporation, or C corporation.

LLC Disadvantages Compared to Sole Proprietorship:

Complexity and Cost: Forming and maintaining an LLC involves more paperwork and higher costs than a sole proprietorship, which has minimal regulatory requirements and costs.

2. LLC vs. Partnership

Partnership: A business owned by two or more individuals. Partnerships come in two main types: general partnerships and limited partnerships.

LLC Advantages Over Partnership:

Limited Liability: In a general partnership, partners are personally liable for business debts and obligations. An LLC provides limited liability protection, safeguarding personal assets.

Management Flexibility: LLCs offer greater flexibility in management and profit distribution, allowing members to tailor arrangements to their specific needs and contributions.

Tax Flexibility: Like partnerships, LLCs benefit from pass-through taxation, but they also offer additional tax options, providing more strategic tax planning opportunities.

LLC Disadvantages Compared to Partnership:

Formation and Maintenance Costs: Establishing an LLC typically involves higher initial formation costs and ongoing fees compared to a general partnership, which has fewer regulatory requirements.

3. LLC vs. Corporation

Corporation: A legal entity that is separate from its owners, with its own rights and obligations. Corporations can be either C corporations or S corporations.

LLC Advantages Over Corporation:

Simplicity and Flexibility: LLCs are generally easier to form and maintain than corporations, with fewer regulatory requirements and more flexible management structures.

Pass-Through Taxation: While S corporations also benefit from pass-through taxation, C corporations face double taxation. LLCs avoid this by allowing profits to be taxed only at the individual level.

Less Formality: Corporations are required to adhere to strict formalities, such as holding regular board meetings and maintaining detailed records. LLCs have fewer formal requirements, making them simpler to manage.

LLC Disadvantages Compared to Corporation:

Access to Capital: Corporations can raise capital more easily through the sale of stock. LLCs cannot issue stock, which can limit their ability to attract large-scale investment.

Prestige and Perception: In some industries, corporations are viewed as more prestigious and stable than LLCs, potentially influencing client and investor perceptions.

Potential Tax Benefits: C corporations can offer certain tax benefits, such as deductions for employee benefits, that are not available to LLCs.

Each business structure offers unique benefits and challenges. The LLC stands out for its combination of limited liability protection, tax flexibility, and management simplicity, making it an attractive option for many entrepreneurs. However, it is essential to weigh these advantages against the potential downsides, such as higher formation costs and limited access to capital, especially in comparison to sole proprietorships, partnerships, and corporations.

By understanding the differences between these business structures, you can make a more informed decision about which one aligns best with your business goals and operational needs. In the following chapters, we will dive deeper into the practical steps of planning, forming, and managing an LLC, providing you with the knowledge and tools to successfully navigate your entrepreneurial journey.

Chapter 2: Planning Your LLC

2.1 Is an LLC Right for You?

D eciding on the right business structure is a crucial step in planning your business. While an LLC offers many benefits, it's essential to determine whether it aligns with your specific needs and goals. This section will help you assess if forming an LLC is the right choice for your business.

Understanding Your Business Needs

Before deciding on an LLC, consider your business's unique characteristics and requirements. Here are some key factors to evaluate:

Liability Protection

Consideration: Do you need to protect your personal assets from business liabilities?

LLC Benefit: LLCs provide limited liability protection, meaning your personal assets are generally safeguarded against business debts and legal actions.

Tax Flexibility

Consideration: Are you looking for tax flexibility and potential tax savings?

LLC Benefit: LLCs offer pass-through taxation, where business income is reported on your personal tax return, avoiding double taxation. Additionally, LLCs can choose to be taxed as a sole proprietorship, partnership, S corporation, or C corporation, depending on what is most advantageous.

Management and Control

Consideration: Do you prefer a flexible management structure without strict formalities?

LLC Benefit: LLCs allow for flexible management arrangements. You can manage the LLC yourself (member-managed) or appoint managers (manager-managed). This flexibility lets you tailor the management to suit your preferences and business needs.

Business Credibility

Consideration: Is enhancing your business's credibility and professional image important?

LLC Benefit: Forming an LLC can enhance your business's credibility with customers, suppliers, and investors, giving it a more professional and established appearance.

Growth and Investment

Consideration: Do you plan to seek outside investment or expand significantly in the future?

LLC Consideration: While LLCs can attract investors by bringing in new members, they cannot issue stock like corporations. If you anticipate needing substantial investment, a corporation might be a better option.

Types of Businesses Suited for LLCs

LLCs are versatile and can be suitable for various types of businesses. Here are some common scenarios where an LLC might be the right choice:

Small Businesses and Startups

LLCs are ideal for small businesses and startups looking for liability protection and tax benefits without the complexity of a corporation.

Professional Services

Consultants, freelancers, and other professionals often form LLCs to gain liability protection and tax advantages while maintaining a flexible management structure.

Real Estate Holdings

Real estate investors frequently use LLCs to hold and manage property, protecting their personal assets from potential liabilities related to the property.

Family-Owned Businesses

Family-owned businesses benefit from the straightforward structure and operational flexibility of an LLC, making it easier to manage and distribute profits among family members.

When an LLC Might Not Be the Best Fit

While LLCs offer many advantages, there are situations where another business structure might be more appropriate:

Seeking Venture Capital

If you plan to seek venture capital or significant outside investment, a corporation might be a better fit due to its ability to issue stock and attract investors more easily.

High Compliance Requirements

Some industries or contracts may require the formal structure and perceived stability of a corporation. In such cases, the additional compliance and formalities of a corporation might be necessary.

Personal Preference for Sole Proprietorship

If you prefer the simplicity and minimal regulatory requirements of a sole proprietorship and are comfortable with the associated personal liability, this might be a suitable option for your small business.

Deciding whether an LLC is right for you involves careful consideration of your business needs, goals, and growth plans. The LLC structure offers significant benefits, including liability protection, tax flexibility, and management simplicity, making it an attractive option for many entrepreneurs. However, it's essential to weigh these advantages against your specific business requirements and long-term objectives.

2.2 Defining Your Business Goals

Setting clear business goals is a fundamental step in planning your LLC. Well-defined goals provide direction, motivate you and your team, and serve as a benchmark for measuring success. This section will guide you through the process of defining your business goals, ensuring that you lay a strong foundation for your LLC's growth and success.

Understanding the Importance of Business Goals

Business goals are specific, measurable objectives that your company aims to achieve over a defined period. They help you:

Clarify Your Vision: Establishing what you want your business to achieve.

Focus Your Efforts: Directing your resources and activities toward achieving specific outcomes.

Measure Progress: Providing a way to track and evaluate your business's performance.

Motivate and Inspire: Encouraging you and your team to strive toward common objectives.

Types of Business Goals

Business goals can be categorized into several types, each serving a unique purpose. Here are the main categories:

Short-Term Goals

Definition: Objectives to be achieved within a year.

Examples: Launching a new product, reaching a sales target, hiring key employees.

Medium-Term Goals

Definition: Objectives set for one to three years.

Examples: Expanding to new markets, increasing market share, developing new services.

Long-Term Goals

Definition: Objectives aimed at achieving over three years or more.

Examples: Becoming a market leader, achieving sustainable growth, expanding internationally.

Financial Goals

Definition: Objectives related to the financial performance of your business.

Examples: Increasing revenue, improving profit margins, securing funding.

Operational Goals

Definition: Objectives focused on the day-to-day operations of your business.

Examples: Enhancing customer service, streamlining processes, adopting new technologies.

Strategic Goals

Definition: Long-term objectives that align with your overall business strategy.

Examples: Building brand recognition, creating strategic partnerships, driving innovation.

Setting SMART Goals

To ensure your business goals are effective, use the SMART criteria:

Specific: Clearly define what you want to achieve.

Example: Instead of "increase sales," set a goal to "increase sales by 20% within the next year."

Measurable: Ensure you can track your progress and measure the outcome.

Example: "Acquire 50 new customers in the next six months."

Achievable: Set realistic goals that are attainable.

Example: "Reduce operating costs by 10% over the next year."

Relevant: Align your goals with your overall business objectives.

Example: "Develop a new product line that complements our existing offerings."

Time-Bound: Set a clear deadline for achieving your goals.

Example: "Launch the new website by the end of the first quarter."

Creating an Action Plan

Once you've defined your goals, create an action plan to achieve them. Here's how:

Break Down Goals into Tasks: Divide each goal into smaller, manageable tasks.

Example: If your goal is to launch a new product, tasks might include market research, product development, and marketing.

Assign Responsibilities: Determine who will be responsible for each task.

Example: Assign team members specific roles in the product development process.

Set Deadlines: Establish deadlines for each task to ensure timely progress.

Example: Set a deadline for completing market research within the first two months.

Monitor Progress: Regularly review progress and make adjustments as needed.

Example: Hold weekly meetings to track progress and address any challenges.

Aligning Goals with Your LLC's Mission and Vision

Ensure that your business goals align with your LLC's mission and vision. Your mission statement defines your company's purpose, while your vision statement outlines your long-term aspirations. Aligning goals with these statements helps maintain focus and consistency.

Mission Statement Example: "To provide innovative tech solutions that enhance small business efficiency."

Vision Statement Example: "To be the leading provider of small business technology solutions globally."

Conclusion

Defining your business goals is a crucial step in planning your LLC. Clear, SMART goals provide direction, motivate your team, and serve as benchmarks for success. By setting and aligning your goals with your mission and vision, and creating a detailed action plan, you lay a strong foundation for your LLC's growth and prosperity.

2.3 Naming Your LLC

Choosing the right name for your LLC is a critical step in the planning process. Your business name is more than just a label—it's a key component of your brand identity and can significantly impact your business's success. This section will guide you through the considerations and steps involved in naming your LLC, ensuring that your chosen name is both impactful and compliant with legal requirements.

Importance of a Strong Business Name

A strong business name can:

Attract Customers: A memorable and descriptive name can draw attention and attract potential customers.

Reflect Your Brand: Your name should convey the essence of your business and its values.

Enhance Credibility: A professional name can enhance your business's credibility and trustworthiness.

Key Considerations for Naming Your LLC

When selecting a name for your LLC, consider the following factors:

Uniqueness

Requirement: Your LLC name must be unique and distinguishable from existing businesses in your state.

Action: Conduct a thorough search of your state's business name database to ensure your chosen name isn't already in use.

Compliance with State Regulations

Requirement: Each state has specific rules regarding LLC names. Generally, the name must include a designator such as "LLC," "L.L.C.," or "Limited Liability Company."

Action: Review your state's naming requirements to ensure compliance. This typically involves checking your state's Secretary of State website or business registration office.

Descriptiveness

Requirement: Your name should give potential customers an idea of what your business does.

Action: Choose a name that is descriptive yet concise, clearly reflecting your products or services.

Memorability

Requirement: A memorable name is easier for customers to recall and recommend.

Action: Opt for a name that is simple, easy to pronounce, and easy to spell.

Domain Availability

Requirement: In today's digital age, having a matching domain name is crucial for online presence.

Action: Check the availability of your desired domain name and secure it as soon as possible.

Steps to Naming Your LLC

Follow these steps to ensure you select an effective and compliant name for your LLC:

Brainstorming

Activity: Generate a list of potential names by brainstorming ideas that reflect your business's mission, values, and services.

Tip: Involve your team or trusted advisors in the brainstorming process to gather diverse perspectives.

Preliminary Search

Activity: Conduct an initial search online to check for existing businesses with similar names. This helps avoid potential trademark issues and ensures uniqueness.

Tool: Use search engines and social media platforms for this preliminary check.

State Database Search

Activity: Search your state's business name database to confirm the availability of your chosen name.

Resource: Visit your state's Secretary of State website or business registration office for the search tool.

Trademark Search

Activity: Perform a trademark search to ensure your chosen name isn't already trademarked by another business.

Resource: Use the United States Patent and Trademark Office (USPTO) online database for trademark searches.

Domain Name Check

Activity: Check the availability of your desired domain name and register it.

Resource: Use domain registration websites like GoDaddy, Namecheap, or Google Domains.

Name Reservation (Optional)

Activity: If you're not ready to file your LLC formation documents immediately, consider reserving your chosen name to ensure it's held for you.

Action: Contact your state's business registration office to learn about the name reservation process and fees.

Finalizing Your Name

Activity: Once you've verified the availability and compliance of your chosen name, finalize your decision.

Tip: Double-check spelling and formatting to avoid any errors in official documents.

Registering Your Name

Activity: Include your chosen name in your Articles of Organization when you file to form your LLC.

Action: Follow your state's specific filing procedures to officially register your LLC name.

Naming your LLC is a vital step that requires careful consideration and thorough research. A well-chosen name can enhance your brand identity, attract customers, and ensure legal compliance. By following the outlined steps and considering key factors such as uniqueness, compliance, descriptiveness, memorability, and domain availability, you can select a name that sets the foundation for your LLC's success.

2.4 Choosing a Registered Agent

Selecting a registered agent is a critical component of establishing and maintaining your LLC. A registered agent plays a crucial role in ensuring your business remains compliant with state regulations and is promptly informed of any legal actions or important documents. This section will explain the role of a registered agent, the criteria for choosing one, and the benefits of making an informed decision.

Understanding the Role of a Registered Agent

A registered agent is an individual or a business entity designated to receive official correspondence on behalf of your LLC. This includes legal documents, tax notices, and compliance-related information. The registered agent must have a physical address in the state where your LLC is registered and be available during regular business hours to accept service of process.

Key Responsibilities of a Registered Agent

Receiving Legal Documents

The registered agent receives service of process notices, such as lawsuits or summonses, ensuring your LLC is promptly notified of legal actions.

Handling Official Correspondence

The agent manages communications from the state, including annual report reminders, tax forms, and renewal notices.

Maintaining Compliance

The registered agent helps ensure that your LLC remains in good standing by forwarding compliance-related documents and deadlines to the appropriate parties within your business.

Criteria for Choosing a Registered Agent

When selecting a registered agent for your LLC, consider the following criteria:

Availability

Requirement: The registered agent must be available during standard business hours to receive documents in person.

Action: Ensure the agent can consistently fulfill this role without gaps in availability.

Physical Address in State

Requirement: The agent must have a physical street address (not a P.O. Box) in the state where your LLC is registered.

Action: Verify that the agent's address meets this requirement and is a stable, permanent location.

Reliability

Requirement: The agent must reliably forward documents to you promptly and securely.

Action: Check the agent's reputation, customer reviews, and track record for reliability and professionalism.

Experience and Expertise

Requirement: The agent should have experience handling legal and official documents for businesses.

Action: Consider agents with a history of providing registered agent services and expertise in compliance matters.

Privacy and Security

Requirement: The agent should ensure your business's privacy and the secure handling of sensitive documents.

Action: Evaluate the agent's procedures for document handling and confidentiality.

Benefits of Choosing the Right Registered Agent

Compliance Assurance

A reliable registered agent helps ensure your LLC complies with state regulations, reducing the risk of penalties and fines for missed deadlines or overlooked documents.

Peace of Mind

Knowing that important documents will be received and handled promptly allows you to focus on running your business without worrying about missing critical notices.

Professionalism

A professional registered agent adds credibility to your business and can enhance your company's reputation with clients, investors, and partners.

Flexibility

Using a registered agent service allows you to operate your business from any location without needing to be present at a specific address during business hours.

Options for Choosing a Registered Agent

Self-Appointment

Consideration: You or another member of your LLC can act as the registered agent.

Pros: No additional cost; direct control over document receipt.

Cons: Requires availability during business hours; may compromise privacy if your address is listed publicly.

Professional Registered Agent Service

Consideration: Hire a professional service to act as your registered agent.

Pros: Expertise in compliance; consistent availability; enhanced privacy and security.

Cons: Additional cost for the service.

Legal or Accounting Firms

Consideration: Some law firms and accounting firms offer registered agent services.

Pros: Professional and knowledgeable; integrated with other legal or financial services.

Cons: May be more expensive than standalone registered agent services.

Choosing the right registered agent is vital for your LLC's legal and operational well-being. By understanding the role and responsibilities of a registered agent, considering key criteria such as availability, reliability, and experience, and evaluating your options, you can make an informed decision that supports your business's compliance and success.

2.5 LLC Operating Agreement

An LLC Operating Agreement is a crucial document that outlines the management structure, operating procedures, and member responsibilities within your Limited Liability Company. While not always legally required, having a well-drafted operating agreement is highly recommended as it provides clarity and helps prevent disputes among members. This section will explain the importance of an operating agreement, its key components, and steps to create one.

Understanding the Importance of an LLC Operating Agreement

An LLC Operating Agreement serves several important functions:

Defines Roles and Responsibilities: Clearly outlines each member's duties, rights, and obligations, ensuring everyone understands their role within the business.

Establishes Management Structure: Details how the LLC will be managed, whether by members or appointed managers, providing a framework for decision-making and daily operations.

Prevents Disputes: By setting out procedures for handling common issues, the agreement helps prevent misunderstandings and conflicts among members.

Protects Limited Liability Status: Reinforces the separation between personal and business assets, helping to maintain the limited liability protection afforded by the LLC structure.

Complies with State Requirements: Some states require an operating agreement for LLCs. Even in states where it's not mandatory, having one enhances the LLC's legitimacy and professionalism.

Key Components of an LLC Operating Agreement

Introduction

Statement of Formation: Confirms the formation of the LLC and includes the LLC's name, principal address, and purpose.

Members: Lists all members and their ownership percentages.

Management Structure

Management Type: Specifies whether the LLC is member-managed or manager-managed.

Roles and Responsibilities: Details the duties and powers of members or managers, including decision-making authority and operational responsibilities.

Capital Contributions

Initial Contributions: Documents the initial financial or asset contributions made by each member.

Additional Contributions: Outlines the process for any future contributions required from members.

Profit and Loss Allocation

Distribution: Describes how profits and losses will be allocated among members, typically based on their ownership percentages.

Distribution Schedule: Specifies when and how distributions will be made to members.

Voting Rights and Procedures

Voting Power: Defines each member's voting power, often proportional to their ownership interest.

Decision-Making: Outlines the procedures for making major decisions, including required voting thresholds (e.g., majority or unanimous consent).

Meetings

Frequency: Specifies the frequency and type (e.g., annual, quarterly) of member meetings.

Notice and Quorum: Details the notice requirements for meetings and the quorum necessary for decision-making.

Transfer of Membership Interests

Restrictions: Describes any restrictions on transferring membership interests, including rights of first refusal or approval requirements from other members.

Process: Outlines the process for transferring ownership interests, including valuation and transfer procedures.

Dissolution and Winding Up

Events Triggering Dissolution: Lists events that may trigger the dissolution of the LLC, such as unanimous consent of members or a specified event.

Winding Up Process: Details the steps for winding up the LLC's affairs, including liquidation of assets and distribution of remaining funds to members.

Miscellaneous Provisions

Amendments: Describes the process for amending the operating agreement.

Governing Law: Specifies the state law that governs the agreement.

Severability: Ensures that if one provision is invalid, the rest of the agreement remains in effect.

Steps to Create an LLC Operating Agreement

Gather Information

Collect necessary information about your LLC, including member details, contributions, and management preferences.

Draft the Agreement

Use a template or consult with a legal professional to draft the operating agreement. Ensure all key components are included and tailored to your LLC's needs.

Review and Revise

Review the draft with all members. Discuss and revise any sections as needed to ensure clarity and consensus.

Sign and Date

Once all members agree on the terms, each member should sign and date the operating agreement. Keep a copy for each member and one for the LLC's records.

Regular Updates

Periodically review and update the operating agreement to reflect any changes in membership, management, or business operations.

Conclusion

An LLC Operating Agreement is an essential document that provides a clear framework for your business operations and helps prevent disputes among members. By including detailed provisions on management, contributions, profit distribution, and other key aspects, the agreement ensures that all members are on the same page and that your LLC operates smoothly. Taking the time to create a comprehensive operating agreement is a wise investment in the long-term success and stability of your LLC.

In the next chapter, we will explore the steps to forming your LLC, guiding you through the legal and administrative processes necessary to establish your business officially.

Chapter 3: Formation of an LLC

3.1 Steps to Forming an LLC

F orming a Limited Liability Company (LLC) involves several essential steps, each designed to establish your business as a legal entity. This chapter will guide you through the process, providing clear and concise instructions to help you navigate the formation of your LLC successfully.

1. Choose Your State of Formation

The first step in forming an LLC is deciding where to establish your business. While many businesses choose to form in their home state, some may opt for states with favorable business laws, such as Delaware or Nevada.

Considerations:

Home State: If your business primarily operates in one state, forming there can simplify compliance and reduce fees.

Business-Friendly States: States like Delaware offer business-friendly laws and courts experienced in handling corporate disputes.

2. Name Your LLC

Selecting a unique and compliant name for your LLC is crucial. The name must distinguish your business from others and meet state-specific naming requirements.

Steps:

Search for Availability: Conduct a search in your state's business name database to ensure the name is unique.

Compliance: Ensure the name includes a designator like "LLC," "L.L.C.," or "Limited Liability Company" and complies with state naming rules.

Reserve the Name: If needed, reserve the name with your state's business registration office.

3. Appoint a Registered Agent

A registered agent is required for all LLCs to receive legal documents and official correspondence on behalf of the business.

Criteria:

Availability: The agent must be available during normal business hours.

Physical Address: The agent must have a physical address in the state of formation.

4. File the Articles of Organization

The Articles of Organization, sometimes called a Certificate of Formation, officially establish your LLC with the state.

Information Required:

LLC Name and Address: The official name and principal address of the LLC.

Registered Agent Details: The name and address of the registered agent.

Management Structure: Whether the LLC is member-managed or manager-managed.

Duration: The length of time the LLC will exist (perpetual or a specific term).

Steps:

Prepare the Document: Complete the Articles of Organization form provided by your state.

Submit the Filing: File the form with the appropriate state agency, typically the Secretary of State, along with the required filing fee.

5. Create an Operating Agreement

While not always legally required, an operating agreement is crucial for outlining the management structure and operational procedures of your LLC.

Contents:

Member Roles and Responsibilities: Detailed descriptions of each member's duties and rights.

Profit and Loss Allocation: How profits and losses will be distributed among members.

Decision-Making Processes: Voting procedures and authority levels.

Conflict Resolution: Procedures for resolving disputes among members.

6. Obtain an Employer Identification Number (EIN)

An EIN, also known as a Federal Tax Identification Number, is required for tax purposes, hiring employees, and opening a business bank account.

Steps:

Apply Online: Submit an application through the IRS website for immediate issuance of the EIN.

Use Form SS-4: Alternatively, complete and mail Form SS-4 to the IRS.

7. Register for State Taxes and Permits

Depending on your state and business type, you may need to register for various state taxes and obtain specific permits or licenses.

Common Requirements:

Sales Tax Permit: If you sell goods or services subject to sales tax.

Employer Taxes: If you have employees, register for state employer taxes.

Industry-Specific Permits: Obtain any necessary permits or licenses required for your industry.

8. Comply with Ongoing Requirements

Maintaining your LLC's good standing requires compliance with ongoing state requirements.

Typical Requirements:

Annual Reports: File annual or biennial reports with your state.

Franchise Taxes: Pay any required state franchise or business entity taxes.

Renew Permits: Ensure all business licenses and permits are current.

Forming an LLC involves several important steps, each critical to establishing your business as a legally recognized entity. By following this step-by-step guide, you can navigate the formation process with confidence and set a solid foundation for your LLC. From choosing your state of formation and naming your LLC to filing the necessary documents and obtaining an EIN, each step is designed to ensure your business is compliant and ready for success.

In the next section, we will explore state-specific requirements for forming an LLC, providing you with detailed information to ensure compliance with local regulations.

3.2 State-Specific Requirements

Forming an LLC involves adhering to specific requirements that vary from state to state. Each state has its own set of rules and regulations governing LLC formation, which can impact your business's compliance and operational processes. This section will provide an overview of state-specific requirements, helping you navigate the formation process in your chosen state.

Understanding State-Specific Requirements

Every state has its unique approach to LLC formation, encompassing various aspects such as filing procedures, fees, annual requirements, and taxation. Being aware of these differences is crucial to ensure your LLC meets all legal obligations and remains in good standing.

1. Filing Procedures

Articles of Organization: The primary document required to form an LLC is the Articles of Organization (or Certificate of Formation in some states). While the basic information required is similar, the specific details and format can vary.

Standard Information: LLC name, principal address, registered agent information, management structure (member-managed or manager-managed).

State Variations: Some states may require additional information, such as the LLC's purpose, the duration of the LLC, or the names and addresses of the members or managers.

Filing Methods:

Online Filing: Most states offer online filing options through the Secretary of State's website or equivalent agency.

Mail-In Filing: Paper forms can be downloaded, completed, and mailed to the appropriate state office.

2. Filing Fees

The cost of forming an LLC varies significantly across states. Filing fees typically range from $50 to $500.

Examples:

Low-Cost States: Kentucky ($40), Arkansas ($50)

High-Cost States: Massachusetts ($500), Texas ($300)

Additional Fees: Some states may impose additional fees for name reservations, expedited processing, or certified copies of documents.

3. Name Requirements

Each state has specific rules for naming an LLC. Generally, the name must be unique and include a designator such as "LLC," "L.L.C.," or "Limited Liability Company."

Name Availability Search: Most states provide an online tool to check the availability of your desired LLC name.

Name Reservation: If you're not ready to file your Articles of Organization immediately, many states offer the option to reserve your LLC name for a specific period.

4. Registered Agent Requirements

All states require LLCs to designate a registered agent with a physical address in the state of formation. The registered agent must be available during normal business hours to receive legal documents.

State-Specific Requirements: Some states have additional criteria for registered agents, such as being a resident of the state or being authorized to do business in the state.

5. Publication Requirements

Certain states require LLCs to publish a notice of formation in a local newspaper for a specified period.

States with Publication Requirements: New York, Arizona, Nebraska

Publication Details: The notice typically includes the LLC's name, date of formation, principal address, and registered agent information. Proof of publication must be filed with the state.

6. Operating Agreement

While not all states mandate an operating agreement, having one is highly recommended for outlining the management and operational structure of your LLC.

States Requiring Operating Agreements: California, New York (for multi-member LLCs)

Best Practice: Even if not required, drafting an operating agreement can prevent misunderstandings and disputes among members.

7. Annual Reports and Fees

Most states require LLCs to file annual or biennial reports and pay associated fees to maintain good standing.

Report Contents: Typically includes updated information about the LLC, such as the principal address, registered agent, and management structure.

Filing Frequency and Fees: Varies by state. For example, Delaware requires an annual report and fee, while Ohio requires a biennial report.

8. State-Specific Taxation

LLCs may be subject to various state taxes, including franchise taxes, sales taxes, and employment taxes.

Franchise Tax: Some states, like California and Delaware, impose an annual franchise tax on LLCs.

Sales Tax: If your LLC sells taxable goods or services, you must register for state sales tax.

Employer Taxes: If your LLC has employees, you must register for state employer taxes and comply with state labor laws.

Examples of State-Specific Requirements

California

Filing Fee: $70

Annual Franchise Tax: $800 minimum

Operating Agreement: Required

Biennial Report: $20 filing fee

Delaware

Filing Fee: $90

Annual Franchise Tax: $300

Publication Requirement: None

Annual Report: Required

New York

Filing Fee: $200

Publication Requirement: Yes, must publish in two newspapers

Operating Agreement: Required for multi-member LLCs

Biennial Report: $9 filing fee

Understanding state-specific requirements is essential for successfully forming and maintaining your LLC. Each state has unique rules and regulations, from filing procedures and fees to publication requirements and annual reports. By familiarizing yourself with these requirements, you can ensure compliance and set your LLC on the path to success.

3.3 Filing Articles of Organization

Filing the Articles of Organization is a pivotal step in the formation of your LLC, transforming your business idea into a legally recognized entity. This document, sometimes referred to as the Certificate of Formation or Certificate of Organization, establishes the foundation of your LLC. Let's explore the essential components and the process of filing this crucial document.

Choosing and Confirming Your LLC Name

The first step in filing your Articles of Organization is to decide on your LLC's name. This name must be unique within your state and comply with state regulations, including the use of designators such as "LLC," "L.L.C.," or "Limited Liability Company." To ensure your chosen name is available, conduct a search in your state's business name database. This step is vital to avoid any legal issues or conflicts with existing businesses.

Providing the Principal Address

Next, you'll need to specify the principal address of your LLC, which is the primary location where your business operates. This must be a physical street address; P.O. Boxes are generally not accepted. The principal address is essential for official correspondence and legal notifications.

Appointing a Registered Agent

Every LLC must designate a registered agent to receive legal documents and official state correspondence on behalf of the business. The registered agent must have a physical address in the state of formation and be available during standard business hours. You can appoint yourself, another member of your LLC, or hire a professional registered agent service.

Determining the Management Structure

Your Articles of Organization must outline your LLC's management structure, indicating whether it will be managed by its members or by appointed managers. In a member-managed LLC, all members share in the decision-making process. In a manager-managed LLC, members appoint one or more managers to handle the day-to-day operations. Clearly defining the management structure is crucial for internal governance and operational efficiency.

Specifying the Duration of the LLC

You will also need to state the duration of your LLC. Most LLCs are formed with a perpetual duration, meaning they continue indefinitely until dissolved. However, you can specify a fixed term if you intend for your LLC to exist only for a certain period or for a specific project.

Outlining the Purpose of the LLC

While some states require a specific statement of purpose, most allow for a general statement such as "to engage in any lawful business activity for which an LLC may be organized in this state." This broad language provides flexibility for your business activities and future growth.

Signing and Filing the Articles of Organization

Once you have completed the necessary sections, the final step is to sign the Articles of Organization. Depending on your state's requirements, this may include signatures from the LLC's organizers, members, or managers. After signing, submit the document to your state's business registration office, typically the Secretary of State, along with the required filing fee.

Filing Methods and Fees

Most states offer multiple filing options, including online, mail-in, and in-person submissions. Online filing is often the quickest and most convenient method, providing immediate confirmation of receipt. Filing fees vary by state, typically ranging from $50 to $500. Check your state's specific requirements and fee schedule to ensure you include the correct payment.

After Filing: Next Steps

Once your Articles of Organization have been approved, your LLC is officially recognized by the state. You will receive a certificate of formation or similar document confirming your LLC's status. Keep this document in your LLC's records as it may be required for opening a business bank account, applying for loans, or other legal and financial activities.

Filing the Articles of Organization is a foundational step in the journey of forming your LLC. By carefully completing each section and ensuring compliance with state regulations, you establish your business as a legal entity, ready to operate and grow. With your Articles of Organization filed, you can confidently move forward, knowing you have laid a solid groundwork for your LLC's future success.

3.4 LLC Formation Costs

Understanding the costs associated with forming an LLC is crucial for effective financial planning. While the expenses can vary significantly depending on your state and specific business needs, having a clear picture of the typical costs involved will help you budget appropriately. This section will break down the common costs associated with forming an LLC, ensuring you are well-prepared for this essential investment in your business.

1. State Filing Fees

The primary cost of forming an LLC is the state filing fee for submitting your Articles of Organization. This fee varies widely from state to state, generally ranging from $50 to $500.

Examples:

Kentucky has one of the lowest filing fees at $40.

Massachusetts charges a higher fee of $500.

These fees are paid to the state agency responsible for business registrations, typically the Secretary of State.

2. Name Reservation Fees

If you want to reserve your LLC's name before filing the Articles of Organization, you may need to pay a name reservation fee. This is an optional step but can be useful if you are still preparing your documents and want to ensure your chosen name is secured.

Typical Costs: $10 to $50 depending on the state.

3. Registered Agent Fees

Every LLC must have a registered agent with a physical address in the state of formation. You can act as your own registered agent, appoint another member of the LLC, or hire a professional registered agent service.

Professional Service Fees: Typically range from $50 to $300 annually.

Hiring a professional registered agent ensures that legal and official documents are handled promptly and provides privacy if you prefer not to use your home or office address.

4. Operating Agreement Costs

Although not always legally required, drafting an operating agreement is highly recommended. You can create this document yourself using templates, but seeking legal assistance ensures it is thorough and tailored to your specific needs.

DIY Templates: Often free or low-cost (under $100).

Legal Services: Hiring an attorney to draft your operating agreement can cost between $500 and $2,000, depending on the complexity of your business.

5. Publication Fees

Some states require new LLCs to publish a notice of formation in local newspapers, incurring publication fees.

States with Publication Requirements: New York, Arizona, Nebraska.

Publication Costs: Vary widely based on location and newspaper rates, typically ranging from $40 to $200.

6. Business License and Permit Fees

Depending on your industry and location, you may need specific licenses or permits to operate legally. These can include local business licenses, health department permits, or professional licenses.

Cost Range: $50 to $500 or more, depending on the type and number of licenses required.

7. Annual Report Fees

Many states require LLCs to file annual or biennial reports to keep their business information up to date. These reports usually come with a filing fee.

Typical Annual Fees: $20 to $100, though some states may charge more.

8. Franchise Tax

Some states impose a franchise tax or annual LLC tax, which is separate from the state filing fee and annual report fee. This tax is typically based on the LLC's income, assets, or a flat rate.

Examples:

California charges an $800 minimum annual franchise tax.

Delaware has an annual LLC tax of $300.

9. Optional Professional Services

While optional, engaging professional services for legal advice, accounting, and business consulting can be beneficial, especially during the initial formation phase.

Legal and Accounting Fees: Can range from $500 to $5,000, depending on the services required.

Conclusion

Forming an LLC involves various costs that can add up quickly. By understanding and planning for these expenses, you can better manage your budget and ensure that you have the necessary resources to establish your business properly. From state filing fees and registered agent services to operating agreements and annual reports, each cost plays a role in setting up a compliant and well-structured LLC. Being financially prepared for these expenses will help you navigate the formation process smoothly and position your LLC for future success.

In the next chapter, we will discuss how to manage your LLC effectively, covering key aspects such as operational agreements, member roles, and maintaining compliance with state regulations.

Chapter 4: Managing Your LLC

4.1 LLC Operating Agreement Details

An LLC Operating Agreement is the cornerstone of your business's internal framework, outlining the rules and structures that govern how your LLC operates. While some states do not require an operating agreement, having one is highly advisable as it provides clarity, prevents disputes, and ensures smooth management. This chapter delves into the critical details of an LLC Operating Agreement, helping you craft a document that serves as a robust foundation for your business.

The Importance of an Operating Agreement

An Operating Agreement serves several vital functions:

Clarifies Roles and Responsibilities: It defines the duties, rights, and obligations of each member, ensuring everyone understands their role within the business.

Establishes Decision-Making Processes: It sets out procedures for making significant business decisions, reducing the potential for conflicts.

Protects Limited Liability Status: By reinforcing the separation between personal and business assets, the agreement helps maintain the limited liability protection provided by the LLC structure.

Facilitates Smooth Operations: With clear guidelines in place, day-to-day operations run more efficiently, and the business can adapt to changes more readily.

Key Components of an LLC Operating Agreement

Statement of Formation: This section confirms the establishment of the LLC, including its official name, principal address, and purpose. It sets the tone for the document, establishing its legal basis.

Member Information

Ownership Details: List all members and their respective ownership percentages. Clearly defining ownership stakes is crucial for understanding profit distributions and voting rights.

Management Structure

Management Type: Specify whether the LLC is member-managed or manager-managed. In a member-managed LLC, all members participate in decision-making, while in a manager-managed LLC, specific individuals are appointed to handle daily operations.

Roles and Responsibilities: Detail the specific duties and powers of members or managers. This section should outline who has the authority to make decisions, sign contracts, and handle financial transactions.

Capital Contributions

Initial Contributions: Document the initial financial or asset contributions made by each member. This ensures transparency and sets the basis for ownership percentages.

Additional Contributions: Outline the procedures for any future contributions required from members. This could include scenarios where the LLC needs additional capital for expansion or unforeseen expenses.

Profit and Loss Allocation

Distribution Methods: Describe how profits and losses will be allocated among members. Typically, this is based on ownership percentages, but alternative arrangements can be specified if agreed upon by all members.

Distribution Schedule: Specify when and how profits will be distributed. This could be quarterly, annually, or according to another schedule that suits the business's cash flow and operational needs.

Voting Rights and Procedures

Voting Power: Define each member's voting power, usually proportional to their ownership interest. This section should also detail any special voting rights or veto powers.

Decision-Making Processes: Outline the procedures for making significant business decisions, including the required voting thresholds (e.g., majority, supermajority, or unanimous consent).

Meetings

Frequency and Type: Specify the frequency and type of meetings (e.g., annual, quarterly). Regular meetings ensure that all members are informed and involved in key decisions.

Notice and Quorum: Detail the notice requirements for meetings and the quorum necessary for making decisions. This ensures that meetings are properly conducted and decisions are legally binding.

Transfer of Membership Interests

Restrictions: Describe any restrictions on transferring membership interests, such as rights of first refusal or approval requirements from other members. This protects the LLC from unwanted changes in ownership.

Transfer Procedures: Outline the process for transferring ownership interests, including valuation methods and transfer approval processes.

Dissolution and Winding Up

Events Triggering Dissolution: List the events that may trigger the dissolution of the LLC, such as the unanimous consent of members, bankruptcy, or the completion of a specific project.

Winding Up Process: Detail the steps for winding up the LLC's affairs, including liquidating assets, paying off debts, and distributing any remaining funds to members.

Miscellaneous Provisions

Amendments: Describe the process for amending the Operating Agreement. This ensures that changes can be made as the business evolves.

Governing Law: Specify the state law that governs the agreement. This is typically the state where the LLC was formed.

Severability: Ensure that if one provision is invalid, the rest of the agreement remains in effect. This clause protects the integrity of the agreement even if parts are challenged.

Crafting a Comprehensive Operating Agreement

Creating a comprehensive Operating Agreement involves careful consideration and precise drafting. Here are some tips to ensure your agreement is effective:

Use Clear and Concise Language: Avoid legal jargon and ensure the document is easily understood by all members.

Consult Legal Experts: While templates can provide a starting point, consulting with an attorney ensures that the agreement is tailored to your specific business needs and complies with state laws.

Review Regularly: Revisit the Operating Agreement periodically to ensure it remains relevant and reflects any changes in the business or its members.

An LLC Operating Agreement is more than just a legal requirement; it is a vital document that ensures smooth and efficient management of your business. By clearly defining roles, responsibilities, and procedures, the agreement helps prevent disputes and sets a solid foundation for your LLC's success. Taking the time to craft a detailed and well-thought-out Operating Agreement is an investment in your business's future, providing clarity, structure, and peace of mind.

4.2 Managing Members and Managers

Effective management is the backbone of any successful LLC, ensuring that day-to-day operations run smoothly and long-term goals are met. Depending on your LLC's structure, the management can be handled by members or appointed managers. This chapter explores the roles and responsibilities of both members and managers, providing insights into how to establish a robust management system that drives your business forward.

Understanding Management Structures

An LLC can be managed in two primary ways: member-managed or manager-managed. The choice between these structures depends on the size of the LLC, the number of members, and the complexity of the business.

Member-Managed LLCs

In a member-managed LLC, all members participate in the day-to-day management and decision-making processes. This structure is common in smaller LLCs where members are actively involved in the business.

Key Responsibilities of Members:

Decision-Making:

All members share equal responsibility in making major business decisions, such as approving budgets, entering into contracts, and setting business strategies. Decisions are typically made through a voting process, with each member's voting power usually corresponding to their ownership percentage.

Operational Tasks:

Members handle various operational tasks, from managing finances and marketing efforts to overseeing production and customer service. This hands-on involvement can lead to a more cohesive and agile business operation.

Financial Oversight:

Members collectively monitor the company's financial health, ensuring that budgets are adhered to, and financial goals are met. Regular financial reviews and audits may be conducted to maintain transparency and accountability.

Compliance and Reporting:

Ensuring that the LLC complies with state and federal regulations is a collective responsibility. Members must stay informed about filing requirements, tax obligations, and any industry-specific regulations.

Benefits of a Member-Managed Structure:

Direct Control: Members have direct control over business operations, allowing for quick decision-making and implementation.

Involvement and Commitment: Active involvement fosters a strong commitment to the business's success.

Challenges of a Member-Managed Structure:

Potential Conflicts: Disagreements among members can lead to conflicts, especially if roles and responsibilities are not clearly defined.

Time-Consuming: Managing day-to-day operations can be time-consuming, potentially detracting from strategic planning and growth initiatives.

Manager-Managed LLCs

In a manager-managed LLC, the members appoint one or more managers to handle the daily operations and decision-making processes. This structure is often used in larger LLCs or when some members prefer to take a passive role.

Key Responsibilities of Managers:

Operational Management:

Managers are responsible for the day-to-day operations of the LLC, including supervising employees, managing finances, and ensuring that the business runs efficiently. They act on behalf of the members, executing strategies and making operational decisions.

Strategic Planning:

Managers develop and implement business strategies to achieve the LLC's long-term goals. This involves market analysis, competitive positioning, and identifying growth opportunities.

Financial Management:

Managers oversee financial activities, such as budgeting, financial reporting, and investment decisions. They ensure that the business maintains financial stability and profitability.

Compliance and Legal Obligations:

Managers ensure that the LLC complies with all regulatory requirements and legal obligations. This includes filing annual reports, maintaining business licenses, and staying updated on industry regulations.

Benefits of a Manager-Managed Structure:

Expertise and Efficiency: Appointing experienced managers can lead to more efficient operations and professional management.

Focus on Growth: Members can focus on strategic planning and business growth, leaving day-to-day operations to the managers.

Challenges of a Manager-Managed Structure:

Less Direct Control: Members have less direct control over daily operations, relying on managers to execute their vision.

Potential Disconnect: There can be a disconnect between members and managers if communication is not maintained effectively.

Establishing Clear Roles and Responsibilities

Regardless of the management structure, clearly defining roles and responsibilities is crucial for smooth operations. Here are some tips:

Draft Detailed Job Descriptions:

Clearly outline the duties and responsibilities of each member or manager. This helps prevent overlaps and ensures accountability.

Set Performance Metrics:

Establish performance metrics and goals to measure the effectiveness of management. Regular reviews and feedback sessions can help maintain high standards and address any issues promptly.

Maintain Open Communication:

Foster a culture of open communication to ensure that everyone is aligned with the LLC's goals and strategies. Regular meetings, updates, and transparent reporting are essential.

Provide Training and Development:

Invest in training and development programs to enhance the skills and capabilities of members and managers. This can improve overall business performance and adaptability.

Effective management is essential for the success of your LLC, whether it is member-managed or manager-managed. By understanding the roles and responsibilities of members and managers, and establishing clear guidelines and communication channels, you can create a strong management structure that supports your business's growth and stability. With the right management in place, your LLC can navigate challenges, seize opportunities, and achieve its long-term objectives.

4.3 Roles and Responsibilities

Effective management is the key to a thriving LLC, and a clear understanding of roles and responsibilities is fundamental to this success. Whether you are running a member-managed or manager-managed LLC, delineating duties and expectations ensures smooth operations, accountability, and cohesive team dynamics. This chapter will explore the various roles within an LLC and the responsibilities each entails, providing a framework for structured and efficient management.

Member Roles and Responsibilities

In a member-managed LLC, all members share responsibility for the day-to-day operations and strategic decisions. Here's a closer look at what this involves:

Decision-Making Authority

Shared Decision-Making: All members have a say in major business decisions. This includes setting company policies, approving budgets, entering into contracts, and making strategic plans. Decisions are usually made through voting, with each member's vote weighted according to their ownership percentage or as outlined in the operating agreement.

Operational Duties

Hands-On Management: Members actively manage the LLC's daily operations. This could involve overseeing staff, managing client relationships, handling marketing efforts, and ensuring product or service quality. Each member may take on specific operational roles based on their skills and expertise.

Financial Oversight

Monitoring Finances: Members collectively monitor the company's financial health. This includes managing cash flow, overseeing accounting processes, ensuring timely tax filings, and reviewing financial statements. Regular financial audits and reviews help maintain transparency and financial stability.

Compliance and Legal Responsibilities

Maintaining Compliance: Ensuring the LLC adheres to state and federal regulations is a shared duty. This involves staying updated on filing requirements, renewing licenses, and adhering to industry-specific regulations. Members must also ensure that the LLC's activities comply with its operating agreement and state laws.

Manager Roles and Responsibilities

In a manager-managed LLC, members appoint managers to handle daily operations and make business decisions. This structure is often preferred for larger LLCs or when some members wish to take a more passive role.

Operational Management

Day-to-Day Operations: Managers oversee the daily operations of the LLC. They supervise employees, manage client and vendor relationships, handle logistics, and ensure that the business runs smoothly. Effective managers streamline operations and improve efficiency.

Strategic Planning

Business Strategy: Managers develop and implement business strategies to achieve the LLC's goals. This involves market research, identifying growth opportunities, competitive analysis, and long-term planning. Managers must align their strategies with the members' vision for the company.

Financial Management

Budgeting and Reporting: Managers are responsible for creating budgets, managing expenses, and ensuring the LLC's financial health. They prepare financial reports, analyze financial performance, and recommend actions to improve profitability and sustainability.

Regulatory Compliance

Legal Obligations: Managers ensure the LLC complies with all applicable laws and regulations. This includes filing annual reports, maintaining necessary licenses and permits, and adhering to employment laws. Managers also implement internal policies to ensure compliance.

Communication with Members

Reporting and Updates: Managers regularly communicate with members, providing updates on the LLC's performance, challenges, and opportunities. Effective communication ensures that members are informed and involved in major decisions, even if they are not involved in daily operations.

Allocating Responsibilities

To ensure clarity and avoid conflicts, it is essential to allocate responsibilities based on skills, experience, and the LLC's needs. Here are some best practices:

Define Roles Clearly

Job Descriptions: Create detailed job descriptions for each role within the LLC. This helps set clear expectations and accountability. Whether a member or a manager, everyone should know their duties and the scope of their authority.

Leverage Strengths

Skills and Expertise: Assign roles based on individual strengths and expertise. For example, a member with a background in finance might handle budgeting and financial planning, while another with marketing experience oversees promotional activities.

Establish Performance Metrics

Goals and KPIs: Set performance metrics and key performance indicators (KPIs) for each role. Regularly review performance against these metrics to ensure that responsibilities are being fulfilled effectively and to identify areas for improvement.

Encourage Collaboration

Teamwork and Communication: Foster a culture of collaboration and open communication. Regular meetings and updates help keep everyone aligned and allow for the sharing of ideas and problem-solving.

Provide Training and Support

Professional Development: Invest in training and development programs to enhance the skills and knowledge of members and managers. Continuous learning helps the LLC adapt to changes and maintain a competitive edge.

Clear roles and responsibilities are the bedrock of an efficient and harmonious LLC. By defining duties, leveraging individual strengths, and fostering a culture of collaboration, your LLC can operate smoothly and achieve its goals. Whether managed by members or appointed managers, a structured approach to roles and responsibilities ensures that your business runs efficiently, stays compliant, and remains poised for growth.

4.4 Record Keeping and Compliance

Maintaining meticulous records and ensuring compliance with legal requirements are fundamental to the successful management of an LLC. Proper record keeping not only supports smooth operations but also safeguards the LLC's limited liability status and helps avoid legal pitfalls. This chapter explores the essentials of record keeping and compliance, providing practical guidance to keep your LLC in good standing.

The Importance of Record Keeping

Record keeping is more than just a legal obligation; it is a vital practice that ensures transparency, facilitates decision-making, and supports financial health. Well-organized records allow you to:

Monitor Financial Performance: Accurate financial records help track income, expenses, and profitability, aiding in budgeting and financial planning.

Support Tax Filings: Detailed records are essential for accurate and timely tax filings, ensuring compliance with federal, state, and local tax laws.

Facilitate Audits: In case of an audit, well-maintained records provide the necessary documentation to support your financial statements and transactions.

Resolve Disputes: Clear records help resolve disputes among members or with third parties by providing a transparent history of decisions and transactions.

Essential Records for an LLC

Organizational Documents

Articles of Organization: Keep a copy of the filed Articles of Organization, which is the foundational document establishing your LLC.

Operating Agreement: Maintain a current version of the Operating Agreement, outlining the LLC's management structure and operational procedures.

Financial Records

Accounting Records: Keep detailed accounting records, including income statements, balance sheets, and cash flow statements. These records should be updated regularly and reviewed periodically.

Bank Statements: Retain copies of all bank statements and reconcile them with your accounting records to ensure accuracy.

Invoices and Receipts: Preserve all invoices issued and received, along with receipts for business expenses. This documentation supports your tax filings and financial records.

Tax Records

Tax Filings: Keep copies of all federal, state, and local tax filings, including income tax returns, payroll tax filings, and sales tax returns. Retain these records for at least seven years.

Supporting Documents: Maintain documents supporting your tax filings, such as expense receipts, payroll records, and depreciation schedules.

Legal and Compliance Records

Annual Reports: File and retain copies of annual reports or statements of information required by your state. These reports typically include updated information about the LLC's members, managers, and registered agent.

Licenses and Permits: Keep copies of all business licenses and permits required for your operations. Ensure that these licenses are renewed as needed and remain current.

Meeting Minutes: Record and retain minutes of all member and manager meetings, documenting decisions, votes, and discussions. Meeting minutes provide a transparent record of the LLC's governance.

Best Practices for Record Keeping

Organize Your Records

Systematic Filing: Develop a systematic filing system, both physical and digital, to organize and store your records. Label folders clearly and maintain a consistent filing structure.

Digital Backup: Utilize digital storage solutions, such as cloud-based services, to back up your records. Ensure that digital files are secure and accessible to authorized personnel.

Regular Updates

Consistent Maintenance: Update your records regularly, ideally on a monthly basis. Consistent maintenance prevents backlogs and ensures that your records are current and accurate.

Review and Reconcile: Periodically review and reconcile your financial records with bank statements and other supporting documents to identify and correct discrepancies.

Implement Policies and Procedures

Record Keeping Policies: Establish clear policies and procedures for record keeping, including who is responsible for maintaining records, how records should be stored, and how long they should be retained.

Training and Compliance: Train your team on record-keeping procedures and ensure compliance with your policies. Regular training helps maintain consistency and accuracy.

Compliance Requirements

Staying compliant with federal, state, and local regulations is crucial for your LLC's continued operation and legal standing. Key compliance requirements include:

Filing Annual Reports

State Requirements: Most states require LLCs to file annual or biennial reports. These reports update the state on your LLC's current information, such as addresses, members, and registered agents. Failure to file can result in penalties or dissolution.

Paying Taxes

Federal and State Taxes: Ensure timely payment of all federal and state taxes, including income taxes, payroll taxes, and sales taxes. Late payments can incur penalties and interest.

Estimated Taxes: If your LLC has taxable income, you may need to pay estimated taxes quarterly to avoid underpayment penalties.

Maintaining Licenses and Permits

Renewals: Keep track of renewal dates for all business licenses and permits. Ensure that they are renewed promptly to avoid fines and interruptions in your business operations.

Employment Compliance

Employee Records: Maintain detailed records for all employees, including payroll records, tax withholdings, and employment agreements. Ensure compliance with labor laws, such as wage and hour regulations, workplace safety standards, and anti-discrimination laws.

Adhering to Operating Agreement

Internal Compliance: Follow the procedures and guidelines outlined in your Operating Agreement. This includes holding regular meetings, adhering to decision-making processes, and maintaining transparency among members.

Effective record keeping and compliance are critical to the smooth operation and legal standing of your LLC. By maintaining organized records, adhering to regulatory requirements, and implementing best practices, you can ensure transparency, accountability, and long-term success for your business. With diligent attention to these areas, your LLC can navigate the complexities of compliance and thrive in its endeavors.

Chapter 5: Taxes and Finances

5.1 Understanding LLC Taxes

N avigating the world of taxes can be one of the most daunting aspects of managing an LLC. However, with a clear understanding of the tax obligations and benefits associated with your business structure, you can confidently manage your finances and take advantage of potential tax savings. This chapter provides a comprehensive overview of LLC taxation, breaking down the key elements to help you make informed financial decisions.

Tax Classification of an LLC

An LLC is a flexible business entity in terms of taxation. By default, the IRS does not recognize an LLC as a separate tax entity. Instead, it allows the LLC to choose how it wants to be taxed. This flexibility can provide significant advantages depending on your business's size, structure, and goals. The main tax classifications for an LLC are:

Disregarded Entity

Single-Member LLCs: By default, a single-member LLC is treated as a disregarded entity for tax purposes. This means that the LLC's income and expenses are reported on the owner's personal tax return using Schedule C, E, or F (depending on the nature of the business). The owner pays personal income tax on the profits.

Partnership

Multi-Member LLCs: By default, a multi-member LLC is taxed as a partnership. The LLC itself does not pay income taxes. Instead, it files an informational return (Form 1065) and issues a Schedule K-1 to each member, detailing their share of the profits or losses. Members then report this information on their personal tax returns and pay taxes at their individual rates.

Corporation

C Corporation Election: An LLC can elect to be taxed as a C corporation by filing Form 8832. As a C corporation, the LLC pays corporate income tax on its profits at the corporate tax rate. Any dividends distributed to members are taxed again on their personal returns, leading to potential double taxation.

S Corporation Election: Alternatively, an LLC can elect to be taxed as an S corporation by filing Form 2553. This allows profits and losses to pass through to the members' personal tax returns, avoiding double taxation. However, S corporations are subject to certain restrictions, such as a limit on the number of shareholders.

Federal Income Taxes

Pass-Through Taxation

Single-Member and Partnership LLCs: In these default tax classifications, the LLC's profits pass through to the members' personal tax returns. This means that the LLC itself does not pay federal income taxes. Instead, members report their share of the profits or losses on their individual returns and pay taxes accordingly.

Self-Employment Taxes

Self-Employment Tax Liability: Members of an LLC treated as a disregarded entity or partnership are considered self-employed. As such, they are responsible for paying self-employment taxes, which cover Social Security and Medicare. The self-employment tax rate is currently 15.3% on net earnings. Members can deduct the employer portion of this tax when calculating their adjusted gross income.

State and Local Taxes

State and local tax obligations for LLCs vary widely depending on the jurisdiction. It is crucial to understand the specific requirements in your state and locality. Common state and local taxes include:

State Income Taxes

Varies by State: Some states impose income taxes on LLCs, while others do not. The way your LLC is taxed at the state level may differ from federal taxation, so it's important to check with your state's tax authority.

Franchise Taxes and Fees

Annual Fees: Many states require LLCs to pay annual franchise taxes or fees for the privilege of operating in the state. These fees can be based on the LLC's revenue, profits, or a flat rate.

Sales Taxes

Sales Tax Collection: If your LLC sells taxable goods or services, you are responsible for collecting and remitting sales taxes to the state. This requires obtaining a sales tax permit and regularly filing sales tax returns.

Deductions and Credits

LLCs can take advantage of various tax deductions and credits to reduce their taxable income. Some common deductions and credits include:

Business Expenses

Deductible Expenses: Ordinary and necessary business expenses, such as rent, utilities, office supplies, and advertising costs, can be deducted from your LLC's taxable income. Keep detailed records and receipts to support these deductions.

Health Insurance Premiums

Deduction for Members: Members can often deduct health insurance premiums paid for themselves and their families. This can be a significant benefit, especially for self-employed members.

Retirement Contributions

Retirement Plans: Contributions to retirement plans, such as SEP IRAs or Solo 401(k)s, can be deducted, reducing the taxable income of the LLC and providing valuable retirement savings for members.

Home Office Deduction

Home-Based Businesses: If you use part of your home exclusively for business, you may qualify for the home office deduction. This allows you to deduct a portion of your home expenses, such as mortgage interest, utilities, and insurance.

Tax Filing Requirements

Federal Tax Filings

Forms to File: Depending on your LLC's tax classification, you will need to file different federal tax forms. Single-member LLCs file Schedule C with their personal tax returns, while multi-member LLCs file Form 1065. LLCs electing corporate taxation file Form 1120 (C corporation) or Form 1120S (S corporation).

State and Local Filings

Compliance: Ensure you file all required state and local tax returns, including income tax, sales tax, and franchise tax returns. Deadlines and requirements vary by jurisdiction, so it's essential to stay informed and comply with all regulations.

Estimated Taxes

Quarterly Payments: If your LLC has taxable income, you may need to make estimated tax payments quarterly to avoid underpayment penalties. This applies to federal, state, and sometimes local taxes.

Understanding LLC taxes is crucial for effective financial management and legal compliance. By familiarizing yourself with the tax obligations and benefits associated with your LLC's structure, you can optimize your tax strategy and minimize your liabilities. Proper tax planning, diligent record-keeping, and timely filing are essential components of managing your LLC's finances.

5.2 Tax Options for LLCs

One of the most appealing aspects of forming an LLC is the flexibility it offers in choosing how the business will be taxed. This flexibility allows you to select the tax structure that best aligns with your business goals and financial situation. In this chapter, we will explore the various tax options available to LLCs, helping you understand the benefits and implications of each choice.

Default Tax Classification

By default, the IRS does not consider an LLC to be a distinct taxable entity. Instead, it provides options based on the number of members in the LLC:

Single-Member LLC

Disregarded Entity: A single-member LLC is automatically treated as a disregarded entity. This means the LLC's income and expenses are reported on the owner's personal tax return using Schedule C, E, or F. The owner pays taxes on the LLC's profits as part of their personal income, simplifying the tax process.

Multi-Member LLC

Partnership: A multi-member LLC is automatically classified as a partnership. The LLC itself does not pay income taxes. Instead, it files an informational return (Form 1065) and provides each member with a Schedule K-1, detailing their share of the profits or losses. Members report this information on their personal tax returns, paying taxes at their individual rates.

Electing Corporate Taxation

An LLC can elect to be taxed as a corporation, either as a C corporation or an S corporation. This election is made by filing specific forms with the IRS and can provide various advantages depending on the business's needs and goals.

C Corporation (C Corp)

Tax Election: To be taxed as a C corporation, the LLC must file Form 8832, Entity Classification Election.

Double Taxation: A C corporation pays corporate income tax on its profits at the corporate tax rate. If profits are distributed to members as dividends, these dividends are also taxed on the members' personal tax returns, resulting in double taxation.

Advantages: Despite double taxation, C corporation status can be advantageous for larger LLCs planning to reinvest profits into the business, attract investors, or offer employee stock options. Corporate tax rates may also be lower than individual tax rates for higher income levels.

S Corporation (S Corp)

Tax Election: To elect S corporation status, the LLC must file Form 2553, Election by a Small Business Corporation.

Pass-Through Taxation: An S corporation allows profits and losses to pass through to the members' personal tax returns, avoiding double taxation. Members report their share of the income on their individual tax returns and pay taxes at their personal rates.

Requirements and Restrictions: S corporations have specific eligibility criteria, including a limit of 100 shareholders, who must be U.S. citizens or residents. Additionally, S corporations can only issue one class of stock.

Advantages: Electing S corporation status can provide tax savings by reducing self-employment taxes. Members can receive a reasonable salary (subject to payroll taxes) and the remaining profits as distributions, which are not subject to self-employment tax.

Choosing the Right Tax Classification

Selecting the appropriate tax classification for your LLC involves considering various factors, including your business size, profit expectations, and long-term goals. Here are some points to help guide your decision:

Simplicity and Convenience

Disregarded Entity or Partnership: For small LLCs or those just starting, the default classifications (disregarded entity for single-member and partnership for multi-member) offer simplicity and ease of tax filing. These options involve fewer formalities and paperwork, making them suitable for businesses with straightforward financials.

Growth and Investment

C Corporation: If your LLC plans to seek significant investment, reinvest profits into the business, or eventually go public, electing C corporation status might be advantageous. C corporations can attract a broader range of investors and offer various employee benefits, such as stock options.

Tax Savings and Income Splitting

S Corporation: For LLCs that are profitable and want to minimize self-employment taxes, electing S corporation status can be beneficial. By structuring compensation as a combination of salary and distributions, members can reduce their overall tax liability while still complying with IRS requirements.

Compliance and Formalities

Corporate Formalities: Electing C or S corporation status introduces additional compliance requirements, such as holding regular board meetings, maintaining corporate minutes, and adhering to more complex tax filing procedures. Ensure your LLC is prepared to meet these obligations if you choose corporate taxation.

Making the Election

To change your LLC's tax classification, follow these steps:

Consult a Tax Professional

Expert Guidance: Before making any election, consult with a tax professional or accountant who can provide personalized advice based on your LLC's specific circumstances. They can help you understand the implications of each tax classification and choose the best option.

File the Appropriate Forms

Form 8832: Use this form to elect to be taxed as a C corporation or to change from one tax classification to another.

Form 2553: Use this form to elect S corporation status. Ensure you meet all eligibility requirements and file the form by the specified deadline (generally within two months and 15 days after the beginning of the tax year in which the election is to take effect).

Maintain Compliance

Ongoing Requirements: After making your election, comply with all ongoing requirements associated with your chosen tax classification. This includes filing the appropriate tax returns, adhering to corporate formalities if applicable, and keeping accurate financial records.

Understanding the tax options available to your LLC is crucial for optimizing your financial strategy and ensuring compliance with tax laws. By carefully considering the benefits and implications of each tax classification, you can make informed decisions that support your business's growth and financial health. Whether you stick with the default classification or elect corporate taxation, the right choice will depend on your unique business needs and goals.

5.3 Financial Record Keeping

Effective financial record keeping is the backbone of a well-managed LLC. It not only ensures legal compliance but also provides a clear picture of your business's financial health, helping you make informed decisions and plan for the future. This chapter delves into the essentials of financial record keeping, offering practical tips and best practices to keep your LLC's finances in order.

The Importance of Financial Record Keeping

Good financial record keeping is critical for several reasons:

Legal Compliance: Accurate records are required to comply with federal, state, and local tax laws. They ensure you can substantiate your tax returns and avoid potential penalties or audits.

Financial Management: Detailed records help you track income and expenses, manage cash flow, and assess the profitability of your business. They provide the data needed for budgeting and financial planning.

Decision Making: Access to accurate financial information enables you to make informed decisions about investments, expansions, and other strategic moves.

Attracting Investors: If you seek external funding, investors will want to see thorough financial records to assess the viability and stability of your business.

Key Financial Records to Maintain

Income Records

Sales Receipts: Document all sales transactions, including invoices and receipts. These records should include details such as date, amount, and customer information.

Bank Statements: Keep all bank statements and reconcile them with your internal records regularly to ensure accuracy.

Expense Records

Receipts and Invoices: Maintain receipts for all business expenses, such as office supplies, utilities, rent, and travel. Ensure each receipt is clearly labeled with the date, amount, and purpose of the expense.

Credit Card Statements: Retain copies of credit card statements and reconcile them with your expense records.

Payroll Records

Employee Information: Keep detailed records of each employee, including personal details, employment agreements, and salary information.

Pay Stubs and Tax Filings: Document all payroll transactions, including pay stubs, tax withholdings, and filings for federal and state payroll taxes.

Tax Records

Tax Returns: Maintain copies of all federal, state, and local tax returns, including income tax, sales tax, and payroll tax filings.

Supporting Documentation: Keep documents supporting your tax filings, such as receipts, invoices, and financial statements.

Financial Statements

Profit and Loss Statement: This statement summarizes your revenues, costs, and expenses during a specific period, providing a clear view of your business's profitability.

Balance Sheet: This statement provides a snapshot of your business's financial position at a given time, listing assets, liabilities, and equity.

Cash Flow Statement: This statement tracks the flow of cash in and out of your business, helping you manage liquidity and plan for future expenses.

Best Practices for Financial Record Keeping

Organize Your Records

Systematic Filing: Develop a systematic approach to organizing your financial records, both physically and digitally. Label folders clearly and maintain a consistent filing structure.

Digital Tools: Use accounting software to automate and streamline record keeping. Cloud-based solutions offer the advantage of accessibility and security.

Regular Updates

Consistent Maintenance: Update your financial records regularly, ideally on a weekly or monthly basis. This helps prevent errors and ensures your records are always current.

Reconciliation: Regularly reconcile your bank statements, credit card statements, and internal records to identify and resolve discrepancies promptly.

Accuracy and Detail

Detailed Documentation: Ensure every transaction is documented with complete details, including date, amount, and purpose. Accurate records are essential for tax filings and financial analysis.

Receipts and Invoices: Always request and retain receipts for all business transactions. Use digital tools to scan and store receipts electronically for easy access.

Security and Backup

Data Security: Protect your financial records with robust security measures, including encryption, password protection, and secure storage solutions.

Regular Backups: Regularly back up your financial data to prevent loss due to hardware failure, theft, or other unforeseen events. Use cloud storage or external hard drives for backups.

Professional Assistance

Hire an Accountant: Consider hiring a professional accountant or bookkeeper to manage your financial records, especially as your business grows. They can provide expert advice and ensure compliance with tax laws.

Consultation: Regularly consult with your accountant to review your financial statements and discuss any potential issues or opportunities for improvement.

Effective financial record keeping is essential for the success and growth of your LLC. By maintaining organized, accurate, and up-to-date records, you can ensure legal compliance, make informed financial decisions, and position your business for long-term success. Implementing best practices and leveraging professional assistance when needed will help you manage your LLC's finances with confidence and clarity.

5.4 Budgeting and Financial Planning

Budgeting and financial planning are vital components of running a successful LLC. They serve as a roadmap for managing resources, setting goals, and ensuring your business remains financially healthy. This chapter delves into the essentials of budgeting and financial planning, offering practical tips and strategies to help you steer your LLC toward sustained growth and profitability.

The Importance of Budgeting

A well-crafted budget acts as a financial blueprint for your business. It helps control spending by setting limits on expenses, preventing overspending, and ensuring funds are allocated efficiently. Understanding your income and expenses allows you to predict cash flow, ensuring you have enough liquidity to meet obligations and seize opportunities. A budget also helps set realistic financial goals and track progress toward achieving them, providing a clear picture of your financial situation to make informed decisions about investments, expansions, and other strategic moves.

Creating a Budget

The first step in creating a budget is identifying your income sources. List all sources of income, including sales revenue, service fees, interest, and any other income your LLC generates.

Be realistic and consider historical data and market trends when estimating future income.

Next, list your fixed and variable expenses. Fixed expenses are regular, predictable costs, such as rent, utilities, salaries, insurance, and loan payments. List all fixed expenses with their amounts and due dates. Variable expenses, on the other hand, fluctuate based on business activity, such as raw materials, marketing expenses, and travel. Estimate variable expenses based on past trends and anticipated changes.

Remember to include one-time expenses, such as equipment purchases, repairs, or special marketing campaigns. These should be planned and budgeted for separately. Setting financial goals is crucial; define short-term goals you aim to achieve within the next year, such as increasing revenue by a certain percentage, launching a new product, or reducing debt. Establish long-term goals for the next three to five years, such as expanding to new markets, achieving a specific profit margin, or investing in significant infrastructure improvements.

With these components in place, allocate your resources. Prioritize spending that aligns with your strategic objectives and provides the highest return on investment. Finally, monitor and adjust your budget regularly. Review it monthly or quarterly to compare actual performance against projections, and adjust as needed to reflect changes in income, expenses, or business goals.

Financial Planning for Long-Term Success

While budgeting focuses on short-term financial management, financial planning sets a course for your business's future. Effective financial planning involves developing financial projections for the next three to five years, including income statements, balance sheets, and cash flow statements. These projections should be based on realistic assumptions and industry benchmarks. Consider different scenarios—best-case, worst-case, and most-likely outcomes—to prepare for various possibilities and develop contingency plans.

Assess your capital needs for future growth, such as purchasing new equipment, expanding facilities, or funding research and development. Identify potential sources of capital, such as retained earnings, loans, or equity investment. Develop an investment strategy that aligns with your business goals, which could include investing in new technology, diversifying product lines, or entering new markets.

Risk management is also crucial. Identify potential financial risks, such as market fluctuations, economic downturns, or changes in regulations, and evaluate the likelihood and impact of these risks on your business. Develop strategies to mitigate identified risks, such as diversifying revenue streams, maintaining adequate reserves, or securing insurance coverage.

Tax planning is another important aspect of financial planning. Work with a tax professional to develop a tax-efficient strategy that minimizes your tax liability while complying with all regulations. This may involve timing income and expenses, taking advantage of tax credits, and structuring transactions in a tax-efficient manner. Ensure timely and accurate tax filings to avoid penalties and interest, and stay informed about changes in tax laws and regulations that could affect your business.

Lastly, consider succession planning for the future leadership of your LLC. Identify potential successors and provide them with the necessary training and experience to ensure a smooth transition when key members retire or leave the business. Develop an exit strategy that outlines how you will sell or transfer ownership of your business when the time comes, whether selling to a third party, passing the business to family members, or structuring a buyout by current members.

Tools and Resources for Budgeting and Financial Planning

Use accounting software to automate financial record-keeping, budgeting, and reporting. Popular options include QuickBooks, Xero, and FreshBooks. Consider working with a financial advisor or accountant who can provide expert advice and help you develop and implement your financial plans. Stay informed about best practices in financial management by attending workshops, reading industry publications, and participating in online courses.

Budgeting and financial planning are essential for the success and sustainability of your LLC. By creating a detailed budget, setting realistic financial goals, and developing long-term financial plans, you can ensure your business remains financially healthy and well-positioned for growth. Regularly reviewing and adjusting your plans based on performance and changing conditions will help you stay on track and achieve your objectives.

Chapter 6: Legal Requirements and Compliance

6.1 Federal and State Laws

N avigating the labyrinth of federal and state laws is a fundamental aspect of managing an LLC. Compliance is not just about avoiding penalties; it's about fostering a sustainable and reputable business. Understanding and adhering to these laws ensures that your LLC operates smoothly and ethically. In this chapter, we will explore the key legal requirements at both the federal and state levels, providing clarity on how to keep your business compliant.

Federal Laws

At the federal level, several key laws impact the operation of your LLC. One of the primary responsibilities is obtaining an Employer Identification Number (EIN) from the Internal Revenue Service (IRS). This unique number is essential for tax filings, opening bank accounts, and hiring employees. It serves as a social security number for your business.

Taxation is another significant area where federal law plays a role. Depending on your LLC's classification, it could be taxed as a sole proprietorship, partnership, or corporation. Understanding these classifications and their tax implications is crucial. Regularly filing federal income tax returns, paying employment taxes, and understanding your obligations under the Affordable Care Act if you have employees, are all integral to maintaining compliance.

Beyond taxes, federal laws also encompass regulations related to labor and employment. The Fair Labor Standards Act (FLSA) governs minimum wage, overtime pay, and child labor laws. If your LLC engages in interstate commerce, adherence to the Occupational Safety and Health Administration (OSHA) standards is necessary to ensure workplace safety.

State Laws

State laws can vary significantly and often have a more direct impact on the day-to-day operations of your LLC. One of the first state-level requirements is the registration of your LLC. This involves filing Articles of Organization with the state's business division, typically the Secretary of State's office. This document officially establishes your LLC and outlines its basic information, including name, address, and members.

Many states require LLCs to file an annual report or a biennial report. This report updates the state on your LLC's current status, including any changes in membership or address. Failing to file these reports can result in penalties or even the dissolution of your LLC.

State taxes also play a critical role. In addition to federal taxes, your LLC may be subject to state income taxes, sales taxes, and franchise taxes. Each state has its own tax rates and filing requirements, so it is important to understand the specific obligations in the state where your LLC is registered and where it operates.

If your LLC operates in multiple states, you will need to comply with the laws of each state, which may include registering as a foreign LLC. This process involves obtaining a certificate of authority to do business in states other than the one in which your LLC was formed.

Licenses and Permits

Both federal and state governments require various licenses and permits depending on the nature of your business. For example, businesses involved in agriculture, alcohol, firearms, and transportation may require federal licenses. At the state level, licenses can range from general business licenses to industry-specific permits, such as health department permits for food service businesses or contractor's licenses for construction.

Staying Compliant

Compliance is an ongoing process. Keeping up-to-date with changes in federal and state laws is essential. Subscribing to updates from relevant governmental agencies, attending legal workshops, and consulting with legal professionals can help you stay informed.

Additionally, maintaining thorough and organized records of all filings, licenses, and permits is crucial. Regularly review your compliance status and address any issues promptly to avoid legal complications.

Understanding and complying with federal and state laws is a cornerstone of responsible LLC management. By diligently following these regulations, you not only avoid legal penalties but also build a strong foundation for your business. In the next section, we will explore specific compliance issues related to employment law, helping you navigate the complexities of hiring, managing, and retaining employees in a legally compliant manner.

6.2 Annual Reports and Fees

Maintaining compliance with annual reporting and fee requirements is a critical aspect of running an LLC. These obligations, though they may vary by state, are designed to ensure that your business remains in good standing with the state authorities and continues to operate legally. This chapter will delve into the intricacies of annual reports and fees, providing you with the necessary knowledge to manage these responsibilities effectively.

Annual Reports: Keeping Your LLC in Good Standing

Annual reports are a mandatory requirement in many states, serving as a way for the state to keep updated records on LLCs operating within its jurisdiction. These reports typically require you to confirm or update information about your LLC, such as the names and addresses of members or managers, the principal place of business, and the registered agent.

Filing your annual report is more than just a bureaucratic necessity; it's a vital part of maintaining your LLC's good standing with the state. Failure to file on time can result in penalties, fines, or even administrative dissolution, which means the state can revoke your LLC's legal status.

The process of filing an annual report is generally straightforward. Most states offer online filing systems that guide you through the required steps. You will need to provide current information about your LLC, and sometimes you will also be required to pay a filing fee. The due dates for these reports vary by state, but they are often aligned with the anniversary date of your LLC's formation or the calendar year.

Fees: Understanding and Managing Your Financial Obligations

In addition to annual reports, there are various fees associated with maintaining an LLC. These fees can include annual registration fees, franchise taxes, and other state-specific charges. It's essential to be aware of these costs and budget for them to avoid any surprises.

Annual registration fees are charged by the state to keep your LLC registered and in good standing. The amount can vary significantly from state to state. Franchise taxes, despite the name, are not only for franchises but are levied on many types of businesses. These taxes are generally based on the LLC's income, assets, or capital, and the rates can vary widely.

Some states also impose additional fees for specific business activities or for maintaining certain licenses and permits. These can include fees for professional licenses, industry-specific operating permits, and local business licenses.

To manage these financial obligations effectively, it is crucial to maintain accurate and up-to-date financial records. Using accounting software can help you track due dates and ensure timely payment of all fees. Regularly reviewing your financial status and setting aside funds for these recurring expenses can prevent any disruptions to your business operations.

Compliance Strategies

Staying compliant with annual reporting and fee requirements requires a proactive approach. Here are some strategies to help you manage these responsibilities effectively:

Calendar Management: Create a compliance calendar that includes all filing deadlines and fee due dates. This can be done using digital tools or traditional methods like planners and calendars.

Automation Tools: Utilize accounting and compliance software to automate reminders and track your obligations. Many of these tools can send alerts before deadlines, ensuring you don't miss any important dates.

Professional Assistance: Consider hiring a professional, such as an accountant or a compliance specialist, who can help you navigate the complexities of annual reports and fees. Their expertise can be invaluable, especially as your LLC grows and its operations become more complex.

State Resources: Take advantage of resources provided by your state's business division. Many states offer guides, FAQs, and customer support to assist with compliance-related questions.

Annual reports and fees are fundamental components of your LLC's compliance framework. By understanding these requirements and managing them proactively, you can ensure your business remains in good standing with state authorities and continues to operate smoothly. Regularly reviewing and updating your compliance calendar, leveraging technology for reminders, and seeking professional assistance when needed are all strategies that can help you stay on top of these obligations.

6.3 Maintaining Good Standing

Maintaining good standing is paramount for the health and legitimacy of your LLC. Good standing indicates that your LLC complies with all state requirements, which is essential for operating smoothly, protecting your liability status, and ensuring continued business growth. This chapter will guide you through the key aspects of maintaining good standing, providing practical insights to keep your LLC compliant and thriving.

Understanding Good Standing

Good standing is a legal status that confirms your LLC is authorized to operate in the state where it was formed. It means that your LLC has met all the statutory requirements, including filing necessary documents and paying all required fees. When your LLC is in good standing, you receive a certificate of good standing (or a certificate of existence) from the state. This certificate is often required when applying for business loans, entering into contracts, or expanding your business into other states.

Key Requirements for Maintaining Good Standing

To maintain good standing, your LLC must adhere to several ongoing requirements. These include timely filing of annual reports, payment of state fees and taxes, and compliance with other regulatory obligations. Let's explore these in more detail.

Timely Filing of Annual Reports

Annual reports are a critical component of your LLC's compliance obligations. As mentioned in the previous section, these reports update the state on your LLC's current status, including any changes in address, ownership, or management. Ensuring that these reports are filed on time is essential. Late filings can result in penalties and jeopardize your LLC's good standing. Most states provide online filing systems that simplify this process, making it easier to meet deadlines and keep your records current.

Payment of State Fees and Taxes

State fees and taxes must be paid promptly to maintain good standing. These can include annual registration fees, franchise taxes, and other state-specific charges. Keeping track of these financial obligations and integrating them into your LLC's budgeting and financial planning processes is crucial. Late payments can lead to fines, interest charges, and potentially the loss of your LLC's good standing. Using accounting software to set reminders for due dates can help ensure that all payments are made on time.

Compliance with Regulatory Obligations

Depending on your industry and the nature of your business, there may be additional regulatory requirements to meet. This can include obtaining and renewing licenses and permits, adhering to health and safety regulations, and complying with employment laws. Regularly reviewing the regulatory landscape and staying informed about changes in laws and regulations affecting your business is vital. Engaging with professional advisors or legal counsel can provide valuable insights and help you navigate complex regulatory requirements.

Responding to State Correspondence

Another important aspect of maintaining good standing is promptly responding to any correspondence from state authorities. This can include notices about upcoming filing deadlines, changes in regulatory requirements, or requests for additional information. Ignoring or delaying responses to such communications can lead to penalties or administrative actions against your LLC. Establishing a reliable system for managing correspondence and ensuring that it is reviewed and addressed promptly can prevent compliance issues.

Proactive Strategies for Good Standing

Maintaining good standing requires a proactive approach. Here are some strategies to help ensure your LLC remains compliant and in good standing:

Regular Reviews: Schedule regular reviews of your LLC's compliance status. This can include checking for upcoming deadlines, verifying that all fees and taxes are paid, and ensuring that all licenses and permits are current.

Documentation: Maintain thorough and organized records of all filings, payments, and correspondence with state authorities. This documentation can serve as proof of compliance and help resolve any disputes or issues that may arise.

Professional Assistance: Consider working with a compliance specialist, accountant, or legal professional who can provide expert guidance and help you manage compliance obligations effectively.

Education and Training: Stay informed about changes in laws and regulations that affect your business. Participate in workshops, webinars, and other educational opportunities to keep your knowledge current.

Maintaining good standing is a continuous process that requires diligence and attention to detail. By understanding and adhering to the key requirements, such as timely filing of annual reports, payment of state fees and taxes, and compliance with regulatory obligations, you can ensure your LLC remains in good standing. Proactively managing these responsibilities not only keeps your business compliant but also enhances its reputation and operational stability.

6.4 Dealing with Legal Issues

Running an LLC comes with its share of legal challenges. Understanding how to navigate these issues effectively can protect your business and help you maintain its good standing. This chapter will explore common legal issues LLCs may face, providing strategies and insights for dealing with them professionally and efficiently.

Understanding Common Legal Issues

Legal issues can arise in various aspects of your business operations. These may include contract disputes, intellectual property concerns, employment matters, compliance violations, and litigation risks. By anticipating these potential problems and preparing to address them, you can minimize their impact on your LLC.

Contract Disputes

Contracts are fundamental to business operations, governing relationships with clients, suppliers, partners, and employees. However, disputes can occur if terms are misunderstood, breached, or poorly drafted. To avoid contract disputes, ensure all agreements are clear, detailed, and legally sound. Involve legal professionals in drafting and reviewing contracts to ensure they protect your interests. If a dispute arises, seek to resolve it through negotiation or mediation before resorting to litigation, as these methods are often faster, less expensive, and less damaging to business relationships.

Intellectual Property Concerns

Intellectual property (IP) is a critical asset for many businesses, encompassing trademarks, copyrights, patents, and trade secrets. Protecting your IP requires diligent efforts, such as registering trademarks, copyrights, and patents, and implementing policies to safeguard trade secrets. If you suspect infringement of your IP rights, address it promptly by consulting with an IP attorney and taking appropriate legal action to protect your assets.

Employment Matters

Employment-related legal issues are common and can be complex. These may involve disputes over wages, wrongful termination claims, discrimination, harassment, and compliance with labor laws. To mitigate these risks, establish clear employment policies, provide training for managers and employees, and maintain thorough records of employment decisions and actions. Understanding federal and state employment laws is crucial. When issues arise, handle them promptly and professionally, often in consultation with legal counsel specializing in employment law.

Compliance Violations

Staying compliant with federal, state, and local regulations is essential to avoid penalties and legal action. Regularly review your business practices to ensure they align with current laws and regulations. This includes adhering to tax laws, health and safety standards, environmental regulations, and industry-specific rules. Engage in proactive compliance audits and seek guidance from legal professionals to address any identified deficiencies promptly.

Litigation Risks

Despite best efforts to avoid them, lawsuits can occur. Litigation can be costly, time-consuming, and damaging to your business's reputation. To reduce litigation risks, implement risk management strategies such as obtaining adequate insurance coverage, maintaining thorough documentation, and fostering transparent and ethical business practices. If litigation is unavoidable, work closely with an experienced attorney to develop a robust defense strategy and consider alternative dispute resolution methods like arbitration or mediation to resolve issues more efficiently.

Proactive Legal Management

Taking a proactive approach to legal management can help you mitigate risks and address issues before they escalate. Here are some strategies to consider:

Regular Legal Audits: Conduct regular audits of your business practices and documentation to identify potential legal vulnerabilities. This includes reviewing contracts, employment policies, compliance procedures, and intellectual property protections.

Legal Education: Stay informed about changes in laws and regulations that affect your business. Participate in workshops, seminars, and online courses to enhance your understanding of relevant legal issues.

Legal Counsel: Establish a relationship with a trusted attorney who understands your business and can provide timely and relevant advice. Having legal counsel on retainer can be invaluable in addressing issues quickly and effectively.

Clear Communication: Foster open and transparent communication within your organization and with external stakeholders. Clear communication can prevent misunderstandings and disputes, reducing the likelihood of legal issues.

Documentation and Record Keeping: Maintain meticulous records of all business transactions, agreements, and communications. Well-documented records can provide essential evidence in resolving disputes and defending against legal claims.

Conclusion

Dealing with legal issues is an inherent part of managing an LLC. By understanding common legal challenges and implementing proactive strategies, you can protect your business, maintain compliance, and minimize disruptions. In the next chapter, we will explore specific compliance issues related to employment law, providing you with the knowledge to navigate the complexities of hiring, managing, and retaining employees within a legally compliant framework.

Chapter 7: Growing Your LLC

7.1 Business Development Strategies

G rowing your LLC is an exciting and challenging phase that requires strategic planning, adaptability, and continuous effort. Effective business development strategies are essential to expanding your market reach, increasing revenue, and ensuring long-term success. This chapter will explore various approaches to business development, providing practical insights to help you navigate the growth of your LLC.

Understanding Business Development

Business development is the process of identifying and pursuing opportunities that can lead to growth and increased profitability. It involves a combination of sales, marketing, strategic partnerships, and market research. Effective business development strategies are tailored to your specific business model, industry, and target market. Understanding your business's strengths, weaknesses, opportunities, and threats (SWOT analysis) is a crucial first step in developing a robust growth plan.

Market Research and Analysis

Comprehensive market research is fundamental to identifying growth opportunities. Understanding your target market, including customer needs, preferences, and behaviors, allows you to tailor your products or services accordingly. Analyzing market trends, competitor strategies, and industry developments helps you stay ahead of the curve and identify niches where your business can thrive.

Conducting surveys, focus groups, and interviews with existing and potential customers can provide valuable insights. Additionally, leveraging data analytics tools to track consumer behavior and market trends can inform your strategic decisions. This research will help you identify new markets, refine your value proposition, and develop products or services that meet evolving customer demands.

Expanding Your Product or Service Offerings

One effective strategy for business growth is to expand your product or service offerings. Diversifying your portfolio can attract new customers and increase sales from existing ones. Consider developing complementary products or services that align with your core offerings. For example, if you run a fitness center, you might introduce a line of branded fitness equipment or offer nutritional consulting services.

When expanding your offerings, it's essential to maintain high standards of quality and ensure that new products or services align with your brand values. Conduct market tests and gather feedback before a full-scale launch to mitigate risks and make necessary adjustments.

Strategic Partnerships and Alliances

Forming strategic partnerships and alliances can be a powerful way to grow your LLC. Collaborating with other businesses can open new markets, enhance your product or service offerings, and provide access to additional resources and expertise. Look for partners whose strengths complement your own and who share similar business goals and values.

Partnerships can take various forms, such as joint ventures, co-branding initiatives, or distribution agreements. For instance, a software development company might partner with a hardware manufacturer to create integrated solutions for customers. Clear communication, mutual trust, and well-defined roles and responsibilities are critical to the success of any partnership.

Leveraging Digital Marketing

In today's digital age, leveraging online marketing strategies is crucial for business development. A robust digital presence can significantly enhance your visibility, attract new customers, and drive sales. Develop a comprehensive digital marketing strategy that includes search engine optimization (SEO), social media marketing, content marketing, email campaigns, and pay-per-click advertising.

Creating engaging and valuable content that addresses the needs and interests of your target audience can establish your business as an authority in your industry. Utilize social media platforms to connect with customers, promote your brand, and gather feedback. Additionally, investing in data analytics can help you track the effectiveness of your marketing efforts and make informed adjustments to improve results.

Enhancing Customer Experience

Delivering exceptional customer experiences is key to retaining existing customers and attracting new ones. Focus on understanding and exceeding customer expectations at every touchpoint. Provide personalized service, respond promptly to inquiries and feedback, and consistently deliver high-quality products or services.

Implementing a customer relationship management (CRM) system can help you manage customer interactions, track sales, and identify opportunities for improvement. Encourage customer loyalty through reward programs, exclusive offers, and excellent after-sales support. Happy customers are more likely to become repeat buyers and brand advocates who can drive referrals and positive word-of-mouth.

Scaling Operations

As your business grows, scaling your operations becomes necessary to meet increased demand. This involves expanding your workforce, enhancing your infrastructure, and optimizing your processes. Investing in technology and automation can streamline operations, improve efficiency, and reduce costs.

Evaluate your supply chain and inventory management practices to ensure they can support your growth. Consider outsourcing non-core functions or forming strategic alliances to leverage external expertise and resources. Effective project management and clear communication are essential to managing the complexities of scaling your operations successfully.

Business development is a dynamic and multifaceted process that requires a strategic approach, continuous learning, and adaptability. By conducting thorough market research, expanding your product or service offerings, forming strategic partnerships, leveraging digital marketing, enhancing customer experience, and scaling your operations, you can drive sustainable growth for your LLC.

7.2 Marketing and Sales

Marketing and sales are the lifeblood of any business, driving growth and profitability. For your LLC to thrive, it is essential to develop effective marketing strategies and robust sales processes. This chapter will guide you through the principles of marketing and sales, offering practical insights and techniques to elevate your business and expand your customer base.

Crafting Your Marketing Strategy

A well-defined marketing strategy is crucial for attracting and retaining customers. It begins with a deep understanding of your target market. Who are your ideal customers? What are their needs, preferences, and pain points? Answering these questions helps you tailor your marketing efforts to resonate with your audience.

Start by defining your unique value proposition. What sets your LLC apart from competitors? This distinct advantage should be at the core of all your marketing messages. Whether it's superior quality, innovative features, or exceptional customer service, clearly communicate what makes your business special.

Next, choose the right marketing channels to reach your audience. In today's digital world, an online presence is indispensable. Develop a professional website that showcases your products or services, provides valuable information, and encourages visitor engagement. Optimize your site for search engines (SEO) to ensure potential customers can find you easily.

Social media platforms are powerful tools for connecting with your audience. Select the platforms most frequented by your target market and create engaging content that encourages interaction. Consistency is key; regular posts, updates, and interactions keep your audience engaged and aware of your brand.

Email marketing remains a highly effective way to communicate with customers. Build a mailing list by offering

valuable content, such as newsletters, exclusive offers, or downloadable resources. Use email campaigns to nurture relationships, provide updates, and promote products or services.

Content marketing is another critical component. By producing informative and engaging content, you can establish your business as an authority in your industry. Blog posts, videos, infographics, and webinars can educate your audience, address their pain points, and demonstrate your expertise. High-quality content not only attracts potential customers but also improves your search engine rankings.

Developing Your Sales Strategy

A strong sales strategy is essential to convert leads into customers and drive revenue. It starts with understanding your sales funnel – the journey potential customers take from awareness to purchase. Each stage of the funnel requires different approaches to move prospects closer to buying.

Begin with lead generation. Utilize your marketing efforts to attract potential customers, capturing their interest through compelling calls-to-action and landing pages. Offer something of value, such as a free trial, consultation, or resource, in exchange for their contact information.

Once you have leads, the next step is nurturing them. This involves building relationships and trust through personalized communication. Use email marketing, social media, and direct outreach to stay in touch with leads, provide valuable information, and address any questions or concerns they may have. The goal is to move them from interest to decision-making.

Closing the sale requires effective sales techniques. Understand the needs and pain points of your leads, and tailor your sales pitch to highlight how your product or service addresses those needs. Active listening is crucial – by understanding their concerns and objections, you can provide solutions and reassurances. Use testimonials, case studies, and demonstrations to build credibility and trust.

Training your sales team is vital to ensure they have the skills and knowledge to close deals effectively. Provide ongoing training on product knowledge, sales techniques, and customer relationship management. Regularly review and refine your sales processes to identify areas for improvement and ensure consistency.

Leveraging Technology

Technology plays a significant role in modern marketing and sales. Customer Relationship Management (CRM) systems are invaluable tools for managing interactions with potential and existing customers. A CRM system helps track leads, monitor sales activities, and analyze customer data to improve your sales strategies.

Marketing automation tools can streamline your marketing efforts, saving time and increasing efficiency. These tools can automate tasks such as email campaigns, social media posting, and lead nurturing, allowing you to focus on strategic planning and creative activities.

Analytics tools provide insights into the effectiveness of your marketing and sales activities. By analyzing data on website traffic, social media engagement, email open rates, and sales performance, you can identify what works and what needs adjustment. Data-driven decision-making allows you to optimize your strategies for better results.

Building Relationships

At the heart of successful marketing and sales is building strong relationships with your customers. This involves more than just making a sale; it's about creating a positive customer experience that fosters loyalty and encourages repeat business.

Provide exceptional customer service at every touchpoint. Respond promptly to inquiries, address issues with empathy, and go the extra mile to exceed customer expectations. Happy customers are more likely to become loyal advocates who refer others to your business.

Engage with your customers regularly. Use social media, email, and other channels to stay connected, share updates, and gather feedback. Personalize your communication to make customers feel valued and appreciated.

Ask for and act on customer feedback. Whether through surveys, reviews, or direct conversations, listening to your customers' opinions helps you understand their needs and improve your offerings. Demonstrating that you value their feedback and are willing to make changes can significantly enhance customer loyalty.

Effective marketing and sales strategies are critical for the growth and success of your LLC. By crafting a well-defined marketing plan, developing robust sales processes, leveraging technology, and building strong customer relationships, you can attract more customers, increase sales, and drive sustainable growth.

7.3 Scaling Your Operations

Scaling your operations is a critical phase in the growth of your LLC. It involves expanding your capacity to meet increased demand while maintaining efficiency and quality. Successfully scaling your business requires strategic planning, investment in resources, and a focus on processes and systems that support sustainable growth. In this chapter, we will explore the key components of scaling your operations, offering insights and practical advice to help your LLC thrive during this transformative period.

Strategic Planning for Growth

Effective scaling starts with a clear growth strategy. Begin by setting specific, measurable goals for your business. These goals should outline what you aim to achieve in terms of revenue, market share, customer base, and operational capacity. Having well-defined objectives provides direction and helps you focus your efforts on the most impactful areas.

Conduct a thorough analysis of your current operations to identify strengths, weaknesses, and areas for improvement. This analysis should include a review of your processes, technology, workforce, and financial health. Understanding your starting point allows you to develop a realistic and achievable growth plan.

Investing in Technology and Infrastructure

Technology plays a pivotal role in scaling operations. Investing in the right technology can streamline processes, improve efficiency, and support increased production or service delivery. Consider implementing enterprise resource planning (ERP) systems to integrate various business functions such as inventory management, accounting, and human resources. ERP systems provide real-time data and insights that are crucial for making informed decisions during the scaling process.

Automation is another key aspect of scaling. Automating repetitive and time-consuming tasks frees up your team to focus on higher-value activities. This can include automation in areas such as customer relationship management (CRM), marketing, and supply chain management. By leveraging automation, you can enhance productivity and reduce the risk of errors.

Expanding your physical infrastructure may also be necessary. This could involve acquiring additional office space, production facilities, or distribution centers. Ensure that your infrastructure investments align with your growth projections and provide the scalability needed to accommodate future expansion.

Enhancing Operational Efficiency

As your business grows, maintaining operational efficiency is crucial to avoid bottlenecks and inefficiencies. Standardizing and optimizing your processes can help you scale effectively. Begin by documenting your current workflows and identifying areas where improvements can be made. Streamline processes to eliminate unnecessary steps and implement best practices to enhance productivity.

Implementing performance metrics and key performance indicators (KPIs) allows you to monitor progress and identify areas that require attention. Regularly review these metrics to ensure that your operations remain efficient and aligned with your growth objectives.

Outsourcing non-core functions can also contribute to operational efficiency. Tasks such as payroll, IT support, and customer service can be outsourced to specialized providers, allowing your internal team to focus on core business activities. Outsourcing can provide access to expertise and resources that may not be available in-house, further supporting your scaling efforts.

Building a Scalable Workforce

Your workforce is a critical component of your scaling strategy. As your business grows, you will need to attract, retain, and develop talent to support increased operations. Start by assessing your current workforce to identify skills gaps and areas where additional resources are needed.

Recruitment should be strategic, focusing on hiring individuals with the skills and experience necessary to support your growth. Invest in employee training and development programs to enhance their capabilities and prepare them for expanded roles. A strong onboarding process ensures that new hires integrate smoothly into your organization and contribute effectively from the start.

Fostering a positive company culture is essential for retaining talent. As your business grows, maintaining the core values and culture that have contributed to your success becomes increasingly important. Encourage open communication, provide opportunities for career advancement, and recognize and reward employee contributions.

Managing Financial Resources

Scaling operations requires significant financial investment. Effective financial management is crucial to ensure that your business has the resources needed to support growth. Develop a comprehensive financial plan that outlines your projected expenses and revenue during the scaling process. This plan should include budgeting for technology, infrastructure, workforce expansion, and other growth-related expenses.

Consider various funding options to support your scaling efforts. These may include reinvesting profits, securing business loans, or attracting investors. Each option has its advantages and considerations, so choose the one that aligns best with your business goals and financial situation.

Regular financial monitoring and analysis are essential to track your progress and make informed decisions. Implement robust accounting practices and use financial software to maintain accurate records. Regularly review your financial performance against your projections to ensure that you remain on track and can adjust your strategies as needed.

Maintaining Quality and Customer Satisfaction

As your business scales, maintaining the quality of your products or services is paramount. Consistency is key to retaining customer trust and loyalty. Implement quality control measures to ensure that standards are upheld across all areas of your operations. Regularly review and update these measures to address any emerging challenges or changes in customer expectations.

Customer satisfaction should remain a top priority during the scaling process. Continuously gather feedback from your customers and use this information to make improvements. Providing excellent customer service and addressing issues promptly can differentiate your business and foster long-term relationships.

Scaling your operations is a complex but rewarding endeavor that can propel your LLC to new heights. By developing a strategic growth plan, investing in technology and infrastructure, enhancing operational efficiency, building a scalable workforce, managing financial resources effectively, and maintaining quality and customer satisfaction, you can successfully navigate the challenges of scaling and achieve sustainable growth.

7.4 Hiring Employees and Contractors

As your LLC expands, building a capable and committed team becomes essential for sustaining growth and maintaining the quality of your offerings. Deciding whether to hire employees or engage contractors depends on your business needs, goals, and resources. This chapter will guide you through the intricacies of hiring employees and contractors, providing practical insights to help you make informed decisions that support your LLC's growth.

Understanding the Difference: Employees vs. Contractors

Employees and contractors serve different roles within a business. Employees are hired to perform specific tasks or roles within your company and are typically given ongoing, consistent work. They are on your payroll, receive benefits, and are subject to your company policies. Contractors, on the other hand, are independent professionals hired to complete specific projects or tasks. They work for multiple clients, set their own schedules, and are not typically eligible for employee benefits.

The choice between hiring employees or contractors depends on various factors, including the nature of the work, the level of control you wish to exert, and the financial implications. Employees are ideal for roles that require ongoing commitment and alignment with your company culture, while contractors offer flexibility and specialized skills for short-term projects or specific tasks.

Hiring Employees

Hiring employees involves a more formal and structured process, ensuring you find candidates who fit both the role and your company culture. Begin by defining the job requirements and creating a detailed job description. This should outline the responsibilities, required skills, qualifications, and the benefits offered. A well-crafted job description attracts the right candidates and sets clear expectations.

The recruitment process involves several steps: advertising the position, reviewing applications, conducting interviews, and assessing candidates' suitability. Utilize various channels for advertising, such as job boards, social media, and professional networks. During the interview process, assess both technical skills and cultural fit. Consider incorporating practical tests or assessments to evaluate candidates' capabilities.

Once you've selected a candidate, extend an offer that includes the job title, salary, benefits, and other terms of employment. Be prepared to negotiate and ensure that the offer aligns with industry standards and the candidate's expectations.

Onboarding is a crucial step in integrating new employees into your LLC. A structured onboarding process helps new hires acclimate to your company culture, understand their roles, and feel supported. Provide comprehensive training and assign a mentor or buddy to guide them through the initial phase. Regular check-ins during the first few months help address any concerns and ensure a smooth transition.

Engaging Contractors

Contractors offer flexibility and specialized expertise, making them ideal for specific projects or tasks that do not require a full-time commitment. When engaging contractors, it is essential to clearly define the scope of work, deliverables, timelines, and compensation. A well-drafted contract outlines these terms and provides legal protection for both parties.

Finding the right contractors involves identifying the skills and experience required for the project. Utilize professional networks, freelance platforms, and industry associations to source qualified candidates. Review portfolios, conduct interviews, and check references to assess their suitability.

Managing contractors effectively requires clear communication and regular updates. Set expectations regarding deadlines, quality standards, and reporting procedures. While contractors operate independently, maintaining regular communication ensures that the project stays on track and any issues are promptly addressed.

Legal and Financial Considerations

Hiring employees and engaging contractors come with different legal and financial obligations. For employees, you must comply with labor laws, including minimum wage requirements, overtime regulations, and workplace safety standards. You are also responsible for payroll taxes, unemployment insurance, and providing benefits such as health insurance and retirement plans.

For contractors, the legal requirements are less stringent, but it is crucial to correctly classify them to avoid legal complications. Misclassifying employees as contractors can result in penalties and back taxes. Ensure that the terms of engagement align with the criteria for independent contractors as defined by the IRS and state regulations.

Financially, employees represent a fixed cost, with salaries and benefits adding to your overhead. Contractors, however, are variable costs tied to specific projects. While contractors may charge higher hourly rates, they do not incur additional costs such as benefits and payroll taxes.

Building a Positive Work Environment

Whether hiring employees or engaging contractors, fostering a positive work environment is key to productivity and retention. For employees, create a culture that values collaboration, transparency, and recognition. Encourage open communication, provide opportunities for professional development, and recognize and reward contributions.

For contractors, treat them as valued partners rather than just external resources. Respect their expertise, honor the terms of your agreement, and provide feedback and recognition. Building strong relationships with contractors can lead to long-term collaborations and better outcomes for your projects.

Hiring the right talent is crucial for the growth and success of your LLC. By understanding the differences between employees and contractors, conducting thorough recruitment and selection processes, and managing legal and financial obligations, you can build a capable and committed team. Whether through long-term employees or specialized contractors, investing in the right people will drive your business forward and help you achieve your growth objectives.

In the next chapter, we will explore strategies for expanding your market reach, providing practical insights to successfully enter new markets and grow your customer base.

Chapter 8: Protecting Your LLC

8.1 Liability Protection

O ne of the primary advantages of forming a Limited Liability Company (LLC) is the protection it offers its owners from personal liability. Understanding and maximizing this liability protection is essential to safeguard your personal assets and ensure the long-term stability of your business. In this chapter, we will explore the concept of liability protection in detail, providing practical guidance on how to effectively shield your personal assets from business-related risks.

Understanding Liability Protection

The cornerstone of an LLC's liability protection is the legal distinction it creates between the business and its owners, known as members. This separation means that the LLC itself is a separate legal entity, capable of owning property, entering contracts, and incurring debts. Consequently, if the LLC faces financial difficulties or legal challenges, the members' personal assets—such as their homes, cars, and personal bank accounts—are generally protected from being used to satisfy the LLC's obligations.

However, this protection is not absolute. There are certain situations where the liability shield can be pierced, exposing members to personal liability. Understanding these exceptions and taking steps to maintain the integrity of the LLC's structure is crucial for preserving liability protection.

Maintaining the Corporate Veil

The legal separation between an LLC and its members is often referred to as the "corporate veil." To ensure this veil remains intact, members must adhere to several key practices:

Proper Documentation and Record-Keeping: Maintaining accurate and up-to-date records of all business transactions, decisions, and meetings is essential. This includes keeping separate bank accounts for the LLC and avoiding commingling of personal and business funds. Proper documentation demonstrates that the LLC is operating as a distinct entity and not merely an extension of its members' personal affairs.

Observing Formalities: While LLCs are generally less formal than corporations, certain formalities must still be observed. This includes holding regular meetings, recording minutes, and following the procedures outlined in the LLC's operating agreement. Consistently adhering to these formalities helps reinforce the LLC's separate legal status.

Adequate Capitalization: Ensuring that the LLC is adequately funded to meet its financial obligations is crucial. Underfunding the LLC can be viewed as an attempt to defraud creditors, potentially leading to personal liability for the members. Proper capitalization shows that the business is intended to operate independently and sustainably.

Limiting Personal Guarantees

In some cases, lenders or suppliers may require members to personally guarantee loans or contracts. While this can be necessary to secure financing or favorable terms, it also exposes members to personal liability if the LLC defaults on its obligations. To limit this risk, members should carefully negotiate the terms of any personal guarantees and seek to minimize their scope whenever possible. Additionally, building a strong credit history for the LLC can reduce the need for personal guarantees over time.

Insurance as a Safety Net

While liability protection through the LLC structure is a significant safeguard, it is not a substitute for comprehensive business insurance. Various types of insurance can further protect your LLC and its members from financial loss:

General Liability Insurance: Covers third-party claims of bodily injury, property damage, and advertising injury.

Professional Liability Insurance: Protects against claims arising from professional services, such as errors and omissions.

Product Liability Insurance: Covers claims related to defective products that cause harm or injury.

Commercial Property Insurance: Protects the LLC's physical assets, such as buildings and equipment, from damage or loss.

Having the right insurance coverage provides an additional layer of protection and ensures that the LLC can withstand unforeseen events without jeopardizing its financial stability or the personal assets of its members.

Understanding Fraud and Misconduct

Liability protection does not extend to fraudulent or illegal activities. If a member engages in fraudulent behavior, misconduct, or acts outside the scope of their authority, they can be held personally liable for any resulting damages. It is essential for all members to operate with integrity, comply with all applicable laws and regulations, and act in the best interests of the LLC. Establishing a strong ethical framework and internal controls can help prevent misconduct and protect the LLC's reputation and financial health.

Liability protection is one of the most significant benefits of forming an LLC, offering peace of mind to business owners by safeguarding their personal assets from business-related risks. By maintaining proper documentation, observing formalities, ensuring adequate capitalization, limiting personal guarantees, securing appropriate insurance, and adhering to ethical standards, you can maximize the liability protection afforded by your LLC. This proactive approach not only shields your personal wealth but also contributes to the long-term success and stability of your business.

8.2 Intellectual Property

Intellectual property (IP) is a vital asset for any business, including LLCs. It encompasses the creations of the mind—such as inventions, literary and artistic works, designs, symbols, names, and images used in commerce. Protecting your intellectual property is essential to maintain a competitive edge, prevent unauthorized use, and enhance the value of your business. In this chapter, we will explore the different types of intellectual property, how to secure protection, and the strategies to manage and enforce your IP rights effectively.

Types of Intellectual Property

Understanding the various forms of intellectual property is the first step in safeguarding your LLC's innovations and brand identity. The primary types of IP include:

1. Trademarks: Trademarks protect brand elements such as logos, names, slogans, and symbols that distinguish your products or services from those of competitors. By registering a trademark, you gain exclusive rights to use these brand identifiers, preventing others from using similar marks that could confuse customers.

2. Patents: Patents provide exclusive rights to inventors for their new and useful inventions, whether they are products, processes, or improvements to existing technologies. A patent grants the inventor the right to exclude others from making,

using, or selling the invention for a certain period, typically 20 years from the filing date.

3. Copyrights: Copyrights protect original works of authorship, including literary, musical, artistic, and certain other intellectual works. This protection gives the creator exclusive rights to reproduce, distribute, perform, and display the work, as well as to create derivative works.

4. Trade Secrets: Trade secrets encompass confidential business information that provides a competitive advantage, such as formulas, practices, processes, designs, instruments, or a compilation of information. Protecting trade secrets involves maintaining their secrecy through measures such as non-disclosure agreements (NDAs) and internal security protocols.

Securing Intellectual Property Protection

To effectively protect your intellectual property, it is essential to take proactive steps to secure legal recognition and enforce your rights.

Trademark Registration: To register a trademark, you must file an application with the United States Patent and Trademark Office (USPTO) or the relevant authority in your country. The application process involves conducting a trademark search to ensure that your mark is unique and does not infringe on existing trademarks. Once registered, a trademark provides nationwide protection and the ability to take legal action against infringers.

Patent Application: Obtaining a patent requires filing a detailed application with the USPTO or the appropriate national patent office. The application must include a thorough description of the invention, how it works, and claims that define the scope of the protection sought. The patent office will examine the application to ensure the invention is novel, non-obvious, and useful. If approved, the patent grants the inventor exclusive rights for a specified period.

Copyright Registration: While copyright protection is automatically granted upon the creation of an original work, registering the copyright with the U.S. Copyright Office provides additional benefits, including the ability to sue for statutory damages and attorney's fees in the event of infringement. The registration process involves submitting an application, a copy of the work, and a fee to the Copyright Office.

Trade Secret Management: Protecting trade secrets requires implementing robust security measures to maintain their confidentiality. This includes using NDAs with employees, contractors, and business partners, as well as employing physical and digital security measures to prevent unauthorized access. Regularly reviewing and updating security protocols ensures ongoing protection of your trade secrets.

Managing and Enforcing IP Rights

Securing intellectual property protection is only the beginning. Effective management and enforcement of your IP rights are crucial to maintaining their value and preventing infringement.

Monitoring and Enforcement: Regularly monitor the marketplace for potential infringements of your IP. This can involve conducting periodic searches, setting up alerts, and using professional monitoring services. If you identify an infringement, take prompt action to enforce your rights. This may include sending cease-and-desist letters, negotiating settlements, or pursuing legal action if necessary.

Licensing and Collaboration: Licensing your intellectual property to other businesses can generate additional revenue and expand your market reach. A well-drafted licensing agreement clearly defines the terms, including the scope of the license, duration, royalties, and enforcement mechanisms. Collaborating with other businesses through joint ventures or partnerships can also leverage your IP for mutual benefit.

Renewal and Maintenance: Intellectual property rights often require renewal to maintain protection. Trademarks, for example, need to be renewed periodically to remain in force. Patents also require maintenance fees to be paid at regular intervals. Keep track of renewal deadlines and ensure that all necessary fees and documentation are submitted on time.

Educating and Training: Educate your employees and stakeholders about the importance of intellectual property and the role they play in protecting it. Provide training on IP policies, security measures, and the proper use of company IP. Creating a culture of awareness and vigilance helps prevent accidental disclosure and misuse of your intellectual property.

Protecting your intellectual property is a fundamental aspect of securing the future and competitiveness of your LLC. By understanding the different types of IP, taking steps to secure protection, and actively managing and enforcing your rights, you can safeguard your innovations and brand identity. This proactive approach not only prevents unauthorized use but also enhances the value and market position of your business.

8.3 Insurance for Your LLC

Insurance is a critical component of any robust risk management strategy for your LLC. It acts as a financial safety net, protecting your business from unforeseen events that could otherwise jeopardize its stability and growth. Understanding the various types of insurance available and selecting the right coverage for your LLC is essential to safeguarding your assets, employees, and operations.

The Importance of Business Insurance

Insurance provides peace of mind, allowing you to focus on growing your business without constantly worrying about potential risks. By transferring the financial burden of unexpected events to an insurance provider, you ensure that your LLC can recover and continue operations even in the face of significant setbacks. This security is particularly crucial for small businesses, where a single incident could have devastating financial implications.

Types of Business Insurance

Several types of insurance policies cater to the diverse needs of an LLC. Each serves a specific purpose and provides protection against different risks. Familiarizing yourself with these options will help you make informed decisions about your coverage.

General Liability Insurance: This is a foundational policy for any business. It protects your LLC against claims of bodily injury, property damage, and personal injury that may arise from your business operations, products, or services. For instance, if a customer slips and falls on your premises or a product you sell causes harm, general liability insurance covers legal fees, medical expenses, and any settlements or judgments.

Professional Liability Insurance: Also known as errors and omissions (E&O) insurance, this policy is essential for service-based businesses. It protects against claims of negligence, errors, or omissions in the services provided. If a client alleges that your advice or service caused them financial harm, professional liability insurance covers legal costs and damages, safeguarding your LLC's reputation and financial health.

Commercial Property Insurance: This insurance covers the physical assets of your business, such as buildings, equipment, inventory, and furniture, against risks like fire, theft, vandalism, and natural disasters. Whether you own or lease your business premises, commercial property insurance ensures that you can repair or replace damaged assets and resume operations with minimal disruption.

Business Interruption Insurance: Often bundled with commercial property insurance, this policy compensates for lost income and operating expenses if your business is temporarily unable to operate due to a covered event, such as a fire or natural disaster. Business interruption insurance helps you cover payroll, rent, and other ongoing expenses, preventing financial strain during periods of inactivity.

Workers' Compensation Insurance: Required in most states for businesses with employees, workers' compensation insurance covers medical expenses, rehabilitation costs, and lost wages for employees who are injured or become ill due to their job. This policy not only protects your employees but also shields your LLC from potential lawsuits related to workplace injuries.

Commercial Auto Insurance: If your LLC owns or uses vehicles for business purposes, commercial auto insurance is essential. It covers liability and physical damage arising from accidents involving business vehicles, ensuring that repairs and medical expenses are covered. This policy also protects your business from legal claims if your employees are involved in accidents while driving company vehicles.

Cyber Liability Insurance: In today's digital age, cyber liability insurance is increasingly important. It protects your LLC against financial losses resulting from data breaches, cyberattacks, and other cyber incidents. Coverage typically includes legal fees, notification costs, credit monitoring for affected individuals, and expenses related to restoring compromised data and systems.

Choosing the Right Coverage

Selecting the appropriate insurance coverage for your LLC requires a thorough assessment of your business's risks and needs. Begin by identifying the specific risks associated with your industry, operations, and location. Consider the value of your assets, the nature of your services, and the potential liabilities you might face.

Consult with an experienced insurance agent or broker who specializes in business insurance. They can provide valuable insights and recommend policies tailored to your LLC's unique requirements. Additionally, regularly review and update your coverage as your business grows and evolves to ensure that you remain adequately protected.

Managing Insurance Costs

While insurance is a necessary expense, there are ways to manage and potentially reduce your premiums without compromising coverage. Implementing robust risk management practices, such as workplace safety programs, cybersecurity measures, and regular maintenance of property and equipment, can lower the likelihood of claims and result in lower premiums.

Bundling multiple policies with the same insurer can also lead to discounts. Additionally, consider opting for higher deductibles, which can reduce your premium costs while still providing essential coverage in the event of a significant loss.

Insurance is an indispensable part of protecting your LLC from the myriad risks it faces. By understanding the various types of business insurance and selecting the right coverage, you can ensure the financial stability and resilience of your company. This proactive approach not only safeguards your assets and operations but also provides the confidence to pursue growth opportunities, knowing that you are prepared for the unexpected.

8.4 Risk Management

Risk management is a vital aspect of running a successful LLC. It involves identifying, assessing, and prioritizing potential risks to minimize their impact on your business. By implementing effective risk management strategies, you can protect your LLC from unforeseen challenges, ensuring long-term stability and growth. This chapter will explore the principles of risk management and provide practical steps to safeguard your business.

Understanding Risk Management

Risk management is the systematic process of identifying potential risks, analyzing their potential impact, and developing strategies to mitigate or manage them. These risks can stem from various sources, including financial uncertainties, legal liabilities, technological failures, natural disasters, and human errors. An effective risk management plan allows you to proactively address these risks, reducing their likelihood and impact on your business.

Identifying Risks

The first step in risk management is identifying the risks that could affect your LLC. Start by conducting a thorough assessment of your business operations, industry environment, and external factors. Consider risks in areas such as finance, operations, compliance, reputation, and technology. Engaging your team in brainstorming sessions can also uncover potential risks that you might not have considered.

Assessing Risks

Once you have identified potential risks, the next step is to assess their likelihood and potential impact. This involves evaluating how likely each risk is to occur and the severity of its consequences. Categorize risks into high, medium, and low based on these criteria. This assessment helps prioritize which risks need immediate attention and which can be monitored over time.

Developing Risk Mitigation Strategies

After assessing the risks, develop strategies to mitigate or manage them. This involves creating action plans to reduce the likelihood of risks occurring or to minimize their impact if they do occur. For example, financial risks can be mitigated by diversifying revenue streams, maintaining an emergency fund, or purchasing appropriate insurance coverage. Operational risks can be managed through robust procedures, regular maintenance, and employee training.

Implementing Risk Management Plans

With your risk mitigation strategies in place, the next step is implementation. Assign responsibilities to team members for each action plan and establish timelines for completion. Ensure that your team understands the importance of these measures and is committed to executing them effectively. Regularly review and update your risk management plans to adapt to changing circumstances and new risks.

Monitoring and Reviewing

Risk management is an ongoing process. Continuously monitor the effectiveness of your risk management strategies and adjust them as needed. Regularly review your risk assessments and mitigation plans to ensure they remain relevant and effective. Stay informed about changes in your industry, regulatory environment, and market conditions that could introduce new risks or alter existing ones.

Creating a Risk-Aware Culture

Fostering a risk-aware culture within your LLC is crucial for the success of your risk management efforts. Encourage open communication about potential risks and promote a proactive approach to identifying and addressing them. Provide training and resources to help your team understand the importance of risk management and their role in maintaining the company's resilience.

Leveraging Technology for Risk Management

Technology can play a significant role in enhancing your risk management efforts. Utilize software tools and systems to track and manage risks, automate monitoring processes, and generate real-time reports. Implement cybersecurity measures to protect against digital threats, and consider using data analytics to identify patterns and predict potential risks.

Collaborating with External Experts

In some cases, collaborating with external experts can provide valuable insights and support for your risk management efforts. Consider working with risk management consultants, insurance brokers, legal advisors, and industry experts who can offer specialized knowledge and guidance. These professionals can help you develop more effective risk mitigation strategies and ensure compliance with relevant regulations.

Risk management is an essential component of protecting your LLC from the myriad challenges it may face. By identifying, assessing, and mitigating risks, you can safeguard your business's stability and ensure its long-term success. Implementing a robust risk management plan not only reduces potential threats but also provides a solid foundation for growth and innovation.

Chapter 9: Changes and Dissolution

9.1 Amending Your LLC

C hange is inevitable in business. As your LLC grows and evolves, you may find that the original structure or provisions no longer fit your current needs. This is where amending your LLC comes into play. Amending your LLC involves making official changes to its foundational documents, typically the Articles of Organization and the Operating Agreement. Understanding when and how to make these amendments is crucial for ensuring your business remains compliant and operates smoothly.

When to Amend Your LLC

There are several instances when you might need to amend your LLC. Changes in ownership, such as adding or removing members, are a common reason. Adjusting the management structure, updating the business address, or changing the registered agent are other scenarios that necessitate amendments. Additionally, any significant changes in your business operations or goals may require an update to your LLC's documents.

Steps to Amending Your LLC

Amending your LLC is a straightforward process, but it must be done correctly to maintain compliance with state regulations. The first step is to review your Operating Agreement and Articles of Organization to identify the specific changes needed. Once you have a clear understanding of the amendments, you must draft a formal amendment document.

This document should clearly outline the changes you are making. For example, if you are adding a new member, include their name, address, and the details of their membership interest. If you are changing the management structure, describe the new roles and responsibilities.

Next, you need to get approval for the amendments. This typically involves a vote among the LLC members, as specified in your Operating Agreement. Ensure you follow the voting procedures outlined in your agreement, as this will make the amendment process legally binding.

Once approved, you must file the amendment with the state where your LLC was formed. This often involves submitting a form, sometimes called an Articles of Amendment, to the state's business filing agency, along with any required filing fee. The state will review your submission and, once approved, update your LLC's records to reflect the changes.

Updating Internal Documents

After filing the amendment with the state, update your internal documents to reflect the changes. This includes revising the Operating Agreement and any other relevant records. Keeping accurate and up-to-date documents is essential for legal and operational clarity within your LLC.

Communicating Changes

Inform all stakeholders, including members, employees, and key partners, about the changes to your LLC. Clear communication ensures everyone is aware of the new structure, roles, or provisions, which helps maintain smooth operations and trust within your business relationships.

Common Amendments

Understanding common amendments can help you anticipate future changes. Membership changes, such as admitting new members or handling the departure of existing ones, often require amendments. Changing the registered agent or the principal business address is another frequent amendment, as is altering the management structure to accommodate growth or shifts in business strategy.

Benefits of Timely Amendments

Timely amendments ensure that your LLC's legal documents accurately reflect its current status, which is crucial for maintaining compliance with state laws. Accurate records also provide clear guidelines for decision-making and operations, helping to prevent disputes and misunderstandings among members. Moreover, keeping your documents up to date can enhance your LLC's credibility with investors, lenders, and other external parties.

Amending your LLC is a necessary part of managing a dynamic and growing business. By understanding when and how to make these changes, you can ensure that your LLC remains compliant and accurately reflects its current structure and operations. This proactive approach not only helps in maintaining legal integrity but also supports smoother internal and external business relationships.

9.2 Adding or Removing Members

As your LLC evolves, there may come a time when you need to add new members or remove existing ones. Whether you are bringing in new talent, adjusting ownership stakes, or responding to a member's departure, these changes must be handled carefully to ensure legal compliance and maintain the smooth operation of your business. Understanding the process and implications of adding or removing members is crucial for the continued success of your LLC.

Adding New Members

Adding a new member to your LLC can bring fresh perspectives, additional capital, and valuable expertise. However, it's important to follow a structured process to ensure that this transition is seamless and legally sound.

Evaluate and Agree: Before adding a new member, current members should evaluate the potential candidate's contributions and fit within the LLC. This evaluation should consider not only financial investment but also the skills and experience the new member brings. Once a suitable candidate is identified, the existing members must agree on the terms of their membership. This typically involves negotiating the percentage of ownership, profit-sharing arrangements, and the new member's roles and responsibilities.

Amend the Operating Agreement: The next step is to amend the LLC's Operating Agreement to reflect the addition of the new member. This amendment should include details such as the new member's name, ownership interest, capital contributions, and any changes to the management structure. It's essential to document these changes formally to maintain clear and legally binding records.

Vote and Approval: According to the procedures outlined in your Operating Agreement, a vote among the current members is usually required to approve the addition of a new member.

Ensure that this vote is conducted properly and that the decision is documented. This formal approval process helps prevent disputes and ensures that all members are in agreement with the changes.

File with the State: Depending on your state's requirements, you may need to file an amendment to your Articles of Organization with the state's business filing agency. This filing updates the state's records to reflect the new membership structure and ensures compliance with state laws. Be sure to check the specific requirements for your state and submit any necessary forms and fees.

Updating Records: Finally, update all internal records to reflect the new membership. This includes financial records, tax documents, and any other relevant business documents. Clear and accurate record-keeping is essential for maintaining transparency and facilitating future business operations.

Removing Members

Removing a member from your LLC can be more complex and sensitive than adding one. It can occur voluntarily, such as when a member wishes to leave, or involuntarily, due to misconduct or failure to meet agreed-upon obligations.

Voluntary Departure: If a member decides to leave voluntarily, the first step is to review the terms outlined in the Operating Agreement regarding member withdrawal. This agreement typically specifies the process for voluntary departures, including notice requirements and the valuation of the departing member's interest.

Negotiate Terms: Negotiating the terms of the departure is crucial. This includes determining the buyout price for the departing member's ownership interest, which should be based on the valuation methods specified in the Operating Agreement. Both parties should agree on the terms to avoid disputes and ensure a smooth transition.

Amend the Operating Agreement: Similar to adding a new member, the Operating Agreement must be amended to reflect the departure. This amendment should include the effective date of the departure and any changes to ownership percentages and management roles. Ensure that this amendment is documented formally and agreed upon by the remaining members.

Vote and Approval: A vote may be required to approve the removal of the member, especially in cases of involuntary removal. Follow the voting procedures outlined in the Operating Agreement and document the decision. This formal approval process helps maintain fairness and transparency.

File with the State: Depending on state requirements, you may need to file an amendment to your Articles of Organization to update the membership structure. Check with your state's business filing agency to determine the necessary steps and ensure compliance.

Updating Records: Update all internal records to reflect the departure of the member. This includes financial records, tax documents, and any other relevant business documents. Clear and accurate record-keeping is essential for maintaining transparency and facilitating future business operations.

Adding or removing members from your LLC is a significant change that requires careful planning and execution. By following a structured process, you can ensure that these transitions are handled smoothly and legally, maintaining the stability and integrity of your business. Clear communication, thorough documentation, and adherence to your Operating Agreement are key to successfully managing changes in membership.

9.3 Dissolving Your LLC

Dissolving your LLC is a significant decision that marks the end of your business's journey. Whether it's due to retirement, partnership disputes, market conditions, or a shift in business focus, the process of dissolution must be handled with care and precision. Properly dissolving your LLC ensures that all legal and financial obligations are met, protecting your personal and professional reputation and paving the way for future endeavors.

Understanding the Dissolution Process

Dissolving an LLC involves several steps, each designed to ensure that the company's affairs are wound up orderly and legally. The process typically begins with a formal decision to dissolve, followed by notifying relevant parties, settling debts, distributing remaining assets, and filing necessary paperwork with the state.

Making the Decision

The decision to dissolve your LLC usually requires agreement from the majority of the members, as outlined in your Operating Agreement. This agreement often specifies the procedures for dissolution, including the required vote and any additional steps. Ensure that the decision to dissolve is documented in meeting minutes or a written resolution to maintain a clear record.

Filing Articles of Dissolution

Once the decision to dissolve has been made, the next step is to file Articles of Dissolution with the state where your LLC was formed. This document notifies the state that your LLC is officially ending its operations. The requirements for filing Articles of Dissolution vary by state, but generally, you will need to provide information such as the LLC's name, the date of dissolution, and a statement confirming that the dissolution was approved by the members.

Notifying Creditors and Settling Debts

After filing for dissolution, you must notify creditors and other parties of your LLC's impending closure. This gives creditors the opportunity to submit any outstanding claims against the business. It's important to settle all debts and obligations before distributing any remaining assets to the members. Failure to properly settle debts can result in legal complications and damage to your personal and business reputation.

Distributing Assets

Once all debts and obligations are settled, the remaining assets of the LLC can be distributed among the members. The Operating Agreement typically outlines how assets should be distributed, often based on each member's ownership percentage. Ensure that this distribution is documented carefully to avoid future disputes.

Canceling Licenses and Permits

To fully dissolve your LLC, you need to cancel any business licenses, permits, and registrations that were obtained during its operation. This may include local business licenses, state tax registrations, and federal employer identification numbers (EIN). Canceling these permits ensures that you are no longer liable for any future fees or taxes associated with them.

Filing Final Tax Returns

You must file final federal, state, and local tax returns for your LLC. Indicate on these returns that they are the final returns and include any necessary documentation to show that the business is being dissolved. This step is crucial to ensure that your LLC meets all tax obligations and avoids penalties or fines.

Closing Business Accounts

After settling debts and distributing assets, close all business bank accounts and credit lines associated with your LLC. This helps to prevent any unauthorized transactions and simplifies your financial affairs as you wrap up the business. Ensure that you keep records of the final transactions for future reference.

Maintaining Records

Even after dissolution, it's important to maintain records of the LLC's activities for a specified period, usually several years. These records may include financial statements, tax returns, and documentation related to the dissolution process. Keeping these records can be helpful if any questions or legal issues arise after the business has closed.

Dissolving your LLC is a meticulous process that requires careful attention to detail and adherence to legal requirements. By following the steps outlined in this chapter, you can ensure that your LLC is dissolved in an orderly and compliant manner. Properly winding up your business affairs not only protects your personal and professional reputation but also sets the stage for your next venture, whatever it may be.

9.4 Handling Debts and Obligations

As you navigate the dissolution of your LLC, one of the most critical tasks is handling outstanding debts and obligations. Properly managing these responsibilities is essential to avoid legal complications and to ensure a smooth closure of your business. Addressing debts and obligations diligently not only fulfills your legal duties but also helps maintain your professional reputation and financial integrity.

Assessing Your Financial Situation

The first step in handling debts and obligations is to thoroughly assess your LLC's financial situation. This involves taking a comprehensive inventory of all outstanding debts, including loans, lines of credit, vendor payments, leases, and other liabilities. Review your financial statements and consult with your accountant to get a clear picture of your obligations.

Notifying Creditors

Once you have a clear understanding of your debts, the next step is to notify your creditors about the dissolution of your LLC. This notification should be done in writing and include key details such as the effective date of dissolution and instructions on how creditors can submit claims. Providing this notice is not only a legal requirement in many jurisdictions but also a professional courtesy that can help prevent misunderstandings and disputes.

Settling Debts

After notifying creditors, prioritize settling your LLC's debts. Start by paying off high-priority obligations, such as secured loans and tax liabilities, which often carry the most significant legal consequences if left unpaid. Negotiating with creditors can also be beneficial; some may be willing to accept a lower payment to settle the debt quickly. Ensure that all payments are well-documented and that receipts or confirmations are obtained to provide proof of settlement.

Handling Remaining Obligations

Beyond financial debts, your LLC may have other obligations, such as fulfilling the terms of existing contracts or leases. Review these agreements to determine any penalties or requirements for early termination. In some cases, it may be possible to negotiate a favorable exit or transfer the obligation to another party. Addressing these contractual obligations is essential to avoid potential legal disputes that could arise after dissolution.

Distributing Remaining Assets

Once all debts and obligations have been settled, you can proceed with distributing any remaining assets among the LLC members. This distribution should be done in accordance with the terms outlined in your Operating Agreement, which typically specifies how assets are to be divided based on each member's ownership interest. Ensure that this process is transparent and well-documented to prevent future conflicts.

Maintaining Records

Throughout the process of handling debts and obligations, it is crucial to maintain meticulous records. Keep detailed documentation of all payments, settlements, and communications with creditors. These records will serve as important evidence of your efforts to settle your LLC's obligations and can be invaluable if any disputes or questions arise later on.

Legal and Tax Considerations

Consulting with legal and tax professionals can provide valuable guidance during the dissolution process. An attorney can help ensure that you are complying with all legal requirements, while an accountant can assist with the tax implications of settling debts and distributing assets. These professionals can also help you navigate any complex situations, such as disputed debts or unclear contractual obligations.

Personal Liability Concerns

One of the primary benefits of an LLC is the protection it offers against personal liability. However, this protection can be compromised if the dissolution process is not handled properly. Ensuring that all debts and obligations are settled can help protect you from potential personal liability claims. It's also important to be aware of any personal guarantees you may have made for business loans or contracts, as these may still hold you personally responsible even after the LLC is dissolved.

Handling debts and obligations is a critical component of dissolving your LLC. By methodically addressing each financial responsibility, you can ensure a smooth and legally compliant closure of your business. Properly settling debts not only fulfills your legal and ethical obligations but also preserves your professional reputation and paves the way for future business endeavors.

In the next chapter, we will explore post-dissolution matters, including how to handle any lingering issues and prepare for new business opportunities. This will provide you with the knowledge and confidence to move forward successfully after closing your LLC.

Chapter 10: Resources and Tools

10.1 Useful Websites and Online Resources

I n the digital age, an abundance of online resources can help you navigate every aspect of managing your LLC. From formation to dissolution, these tools and websites provide invaluable information, services, and support, ensuring that you have the knowledge and assistance you need at every step.

Official Government Websites

Government websites are often the most reliable sources of information for legal and regulatory matters related to LLCs. The U.S. Small Business Administration (SBA) is a crucial resource, offering comprehensive guides on starting and managing small businesses. Their website provides detailed information on business planning, legal requirements, and financial management. Additionally, the Internal Revenue Service (IRS) website is essential for understanding tax obligations, filing requirements, and accessing necessary forms for your LLC.

Each state has its own business filing agency, typically accessible through the Secretary of State's website. These sites provide state-specific information on forming, amending, and dissolving LLCs. They also offer online services for filing documents, paying fees, and checking the status of your LLC. Familiarizing yourself with your state's business portal can streamline many administrative tasks and ensure compliance with local regulations.

Business Formation Services

Several online platforms specialize in LLC formation and offer a range of services to simplify the process. Websites like LegalZoom, Incfile, and Rocket Lawyer provide step-by-step guidance on forming an LLC, filing necessary documents, and maintaining compliance. These services often include options for registered agent services, operating agreement templates, and ongoing compliance monitoring, making them valuable tools for both new and existing LLC owners.

Educational Resources and Courses

For those seeking a deeper understanding of business management and legal matters, numerous educational websites offer courses and resources tailored to small business owners. Platforms like Coursera, Udemy, and LinkedIn Learning provide courses on business planning, financial management, marketing strategies, and more. These courses are designed to be accessible and practical, helping you acquire the skills needed to run your LLC effectively.

Financial Management Tools

Effective financial management is crucial for the success of your LLC. Online accounting software such as QuickBooks, Xero, and Wave can help you track income and expenses, manage payroll, and generate financial reports. These tools often integrate with your bank accounts and other financial services, providing real-time insights into your business's financial health. Additionally, many of these platforms offer features tailored to LLCs, such as multi-member management and tax preparation support.

Legal and Compliance Tools

Staying compliant with legal requirements is essential for maintaining the good standing of your LLC. Websites like Nolo and FindLaw offer extensive libraries of articles, guides, and templates covering a wide range of legal topics. These resources can help you draft contracts, understand employment laws, and navigate regulatory changes. Additionally, compliance management tools like ComplianceMate can automate reminders for filing deadlines, license renewals, and other critical tasks, ensuring that your LLC remains compliant with minimal effort.

Marketing and Business Development Resources

Building and growing your LLC often requires effective marketing strategies and business development efforts. Websites like HubSpot, Hootsuite, and Canva provide tools and resources for creating and managing marketing campaigns, engaging with customers on social media, and designing professional marketing materials. These platforms offer both free and paid options, making them accessible to businesses of all sizes and budgets.

Networking and Support Communities

Connecting with other business owners and professionals can provide valuable insights, support, and opportunities for collaboration. Online communities such as Reddit's r/smallbusiness, the Small Business Forum, and LinkedIn groups dedicated to entrepreneurs and small business owners offer spaces to ask questions, share experiences, and seek advice. These communities can be particularly helpful for finding solutions to common challenges and staying updated on industry trends.

Leveraging online resources and tools can significantly enhance your ability to manage and grow your LLC. From official government websites and business formation services to financial management tools and educational platforms, the digital landscape offers a wealth of information and support. By integrating these resources into your business operations, you can ensure that you have the knowledge and tools needed to navigate the complexities of running an LLC successfully.

10.2 Recommended Books and Courses

Books and courses can provide in-depth knowledge and practical skills essential for managing and growing your LLC. These resources offer insights from experts, case studies, and actionable strategies, making them invaluable tools for both novice and experienced business owners.

Books

Starting with foundational knowledge, "The E-Myth Revisited" by Michael E. Gerber is a must-read for any entrepreneur. Gerber dispels common myths about starting a business and provides a comprehensive guide to building a business that works for you. The book emphasizes the importance of developing systems and processes to ensure your business can operate smoothly and efficiently.

For those interested in the financial aspects of running an LLC, "Accounting Made Simple: Accounting Explained in 100 Pages or Less" by Mike Piper is an excellent resource. Piper breaks down complex accounting concepts into easy-to-understand language, making it accessible for those without a financial background. This book covers the basics of financial statements, accounting principles, and bookkeeping, which are crucial for maintaining the financial health of your LLC.

"LLC or Corporation? How to Choose the Right Form for Your Business" by Anthony Mancuso offers detailed comparisons between LLCs and corporations, helping you understand the nuances of each business structure. Mancuso provides practical advice on legal and tax implications, making it easier to choose the right form for your business needs.

For insights into business growth and scaling, "Scaling Up: How a Few Companies Make It...and Why the Rest Don't" by Verne Harnish is an essential read. Harnish provides a framework for managing the four major decisions every company must get right: People, Strategy, Execution, and Cash. This book is particularly valuable for LLC owners looking to expand their operations and achieve sustainable growth.

Courses

Online courses offer a flexible and interactive way to gain new skills and knowledge. "Starting a Business" by the University of Michigan on Coursera is an excellent course for those at the beginning of their entrepreneurial journey. It covers essential topics such as business planning, financing, marketing, and legal considerations. The course is designed to provide a solid foundation for launching a successful business.

For a deep dive into financial management, "Financial Accounting Fundamentals" by the University of Virginia on Coursera is highly recommended. This course offers a thorough understanding of financial accounting, including how to read financial statements and analyze business performance. It is an invaluable resource for LLC owners who want to take control of their financial health.

To enhance your marketing skills, "Digital Marketing Specialization" by the University of Illinois on Coursera is a comprehensive program covering topics such as search engine optimization (SEO), social media marketing, and digital analytics. This course is designed to help you develop effective marketing strategies to grow your LLC's online presence and attract more customers.

For leadership and management skills, "Leadership Principles" by Harvard Business School Online provides a deep understanding of effective leadership practices. The course includes case studies, interactive exercises, and insights from top leaders, helping you develop the skills necessary to lead your team and make strategic decisions.

Books and courses are powerful tools that can significantly enhance your ability to manage and grow your LLC. By investing in these resources, you can gain valuable knowledge, develop critical skills, and stay updated on best practices and industry trends. Whether you are just starting out or looking to scale your business, the right books and courses can provide the guidance and support you need to succeed.

10.3 Professional Services: When to Seek Help

Running an LLC can be a complex endeavor, often requiring expertise beyond what you may possess. Recognizing when to seek professional help is crucial for the success and sustainability of your business. Engaging the right professionals at the right time can save you time, money, and potential legal troubles, ensuring your LLC operates smoothly and efficiently.

Legal Services

Navigating the legal landscape of business can be daunting. Consulting with an attorney is advisable from the very beginning, especially when forming your LLC. A lawyer can assist with drafting the Operating Agreement, ensuring it complies with state laws and addresses all necessary contingencies. They can also provide guidance on intellectual property issues, contracts, and compliance with local, state, and federal regulations.

As your business grows, you may face more complex legal issues such as mergers, acquisitions, or disputes with partners or clients. Having an attorney who understands your business and its history can be invaluable in these situations, helping you navigate legal challenges and mitigate risks effectively.

Accounting and Tax Services

Managing your LLC's finances requires meticulous attention to detail. An accountant can help set up an effective bookkeeping system, ensuring that your financial records are accurate and up to date. They can also provide strategic tax planning advice, helping you take advantage of tax benefits and avoid potential pitfalls.

Tax season can be particularly stressful for business owners. A tax professional can prepare and file your tax returns, ensuring compliance with all tax laws and regulations. They can also represent your business in case of an audit, providing peace of mind and allowing you to focus on running your business.

Financial Advisory Services

Beyond basic accounting, a financial advisor can offer insights into the financial health of your LLC and help you plan for the future. They can assist with budgeting, cash flow management, and financial forecasting, enabling you to make informed decisions about investments and growth strategies.

If you are considering expanding your business, acquiring new assets, or entering new markets, a financial advisor can provide valuable advice on the financial implications of these moves. They can help you understand the risks and rewards, ensuring that your growth strategies are financially sound and sustainable.

Human Resources Consulting

As your LLC grows and you start hiring employees, managing human resources can become increasingly complex. An HR consultant can help you develop effective hiring practices, create comprehensive employee handbooks, and ensure compliance with labor laws. They can also assist with performance management, employee benefits, and workplace policies, fostering a positive and productive work environment.

HR consultants can also provide guidance on handling sensitive issues such as employee disputes, terminations, and workplace harassment. Their expertise can help you navigate these challenging situations while minimizing legal risks and maintaining a respectful and lawful workplace.

Marketing and Branding Services

Effective marketing and branding are essential for attracting and retaining customers. A marketing consultant or agency can help you develop a strategic marketing plan, create compelling content, and manage your online presence. They can also provide insights into market trends and consumer behavior, helping you tailor your marketing efforts to your target audience.

Investing in professional branding services can also elevate your business's image. Branding experts can help you create a strong, cohesive brand identity that resonates with your customers and sets you apart from competitors. This includes designing logos, developing brand guidelines, and crafting a consistent brand message.

IT and Technology Services

In today's digital world, reliable IT systems are crucial for business operations. An IT consultant can help you set up and maintain your technology infrastructure, ensuring it meets your business needs and is secure from cyber threats. They can also assist with implementing software solutions that streamline operations, improve efficiency, and enhance customer experience.

As your business grows, you may need more advanced IT services such as data management, network security, and disaster recovery planning. Engaging IT professionals can ensure that your technology systems are robust, scalable, and aligned with your business goals.

Knowing when to seek professional services is a key aspect of successful business management. Legal, accounting, financial, HR, marketing, and IT professionals bring specialized expertise that can address specific challenges and opportunities your LLC may face. By leveraging their knowledge and experience, you can focus on what you do best—running and growing your business—while ensuring that critical aspects of your operations are handled expertly and efficiently.

10.4 Templates and Checklists

Running an LLC involves numerous tasks, from managing finances and complying with legal requirements to marketing and hiring. To help streamline these processes and ensure you don't overlook essential steps, using templates and checklists can be incredibly valuable. These tools provide structure, save time, and reduce the likelihood of errors, making your business operations more efficient and effective.

Business Plan Template

A well-crafted business plan is crucial for defining your business goals, strategies, and roadmap for success. A business plan template guides you through the process, ensuring you include all necessary sections such as executive summary, market analysis, organizational structure, product line or services, marketing strategy, and financial projections. Using a template helps you organize your thoughts clearly and comprehensively, making it easier to present your business plan to investors, partners, and stakeholders.

Operating Agreement Template

The Operating Agreement is a foundational document for your LLC, outlining the management structure, member roles, and operational procedures. An Operating Agreement template can simplify this complex task by providing a framework that covers essential elements such as member contributions, profit distribution, decision-making processes, and procedures for adding or removing members. This ensures that your Operating Agreement is thorough and legally sound, protecting your business and its members.

Financial Statements and Budget Templates

Maintaining accurate financial records is vital for the health of your LLC. Financial statement templates for balance sheets, income statements, and cash flow statements help you track your business's financial performance. These templates provide standardized formats, making it easier to record, review, and analyze financial data. Additionally, budgeting templates help you plan and monitor your finances, ensuring you allocate resources effectively and stay on track to meet your financial goals.

Marketing Plan Template

A comprehensive marketing plan is essential for promoting your LLC and attracting customers. A marketing plan template guides you through the development of a strategy that includes market research, target audience identification, marketing goals, and tactics for reaching your audience. By following a template, you can ensure your marketing efforts are well-organized and aligned with your business objectives, helping you maximize your marketing ROI.

Employee Handbook Template

As your LLC grows and you hire employees, having an employee handbook is crucial for setting clear expectations and maintaining a positive work environment. An employee handbook template provides a structure for outlining your company's policies, procedures, and benefits. It typically includes sections on company culture, code of conduct, employment terms, compensation, benefits, and disciplinary procedures. This helps ensure consistency in how you manage your workforce and provides a reference for employees to understand their rights and responsibilities.

Compliance Checklists

Staying compliant with legal and regulatory requirements is critical for avoiding penalties and maintaining your LLC's good standing. Compliance checklists help you track essential tasks such as filing annual reports, renewing licenses, paying taxes, and maintaining proper records. By using these checklists, you can ensure that all compliance-related tasks are completed on time and that you don't miss any crucial deadlines.

Project Management Templates

Managing projects efficiently requires careful planning and organization. Project management templates, such as Gantt charts, task lists, and project timelines, help you break down projects into manageable steps, assign responsibilities, and track progress. These templates provide a visual overview of your projects, making it easier to coordinate efforts, meet deadlines, and achieve your project goals.

Meeting Agenda and Minutes Templates

Effective meetings are essential for making decisions and keeping your team aligned. Meeting agenda templates help you plan and structure your meetings, ensuring that all necessary topics are covered and that the meeting stays on track. Minutes templates provide a standardized format for recording discussions, decisions, and action items, ensuring that there is a clear record of what was discussed and agreed upon.

Conclusion

Templates and checklists are indispensable tools for managing the various aspects of your LLC. They provide structure, save time, and ensure consistency, helping you run your business more efficiently and effectively. By utilizing these resources, you can focus more on strategic decision-making and growth while maintaining organized and compliant operations.

Appendices

A. Glossary of Terms

U nderstanding the language of LLCs is crucial for navigating the complexities of business ownership. Here, we've compiled a concise glossary of essential terms.

An LLC (Limited Liability Company) is a business structure that provides personal liability protection to its owners, known as members. The Operating Agreement is a legal document that outlines the ownership and operating procedures of the LLC. Articles of Organization are the formal documents filed with the state to establish the LLC. A Registered Agent is a person or entity designated to receive legal documents on behalf of the LLC. Dissolution refers to the process of legally closing an LLC. Commingling means mixing personal and business finances, which is a practice that should be avoided to maintain liability protection.

B. Sample LLC Operating Agreement

A well-drafted Operating Agreement is fundamental for your LLC. Below is a simplified example to illustrate the key sections you should include.

Introduction: This section includes the name of the LLC, the date of formation, and the names of the members.

Purpose: Clearly state the purpose of the LLC, whether it's broad or specific to a particular industry.

Membership: Define the roles, responsibilities, and ownership percentages of each member. This section should also cover how new members can be added and the process for a member leaving the LLC.

Management: Outline whether the LLC will be managed by its members or by appointed managers. Include details on decision-making processes, voting rights, and meeting schedules.

Distributions: Specify how profits and losses will be allocated among members. Include information on how and when distributions will be made.

Dissolution: Detail the procedures for dissolving the LLC, including how remaining assets will be distributed after all debts and obligations have been satisfied.

B. State-by-State LLC Resources

Navigating state-specific requirements is crucial for compliance and smooth operation. Each state has unique rules and resources for forming and managing an LLC. For example, in California, LLCs must file an annual Statement of Information, while in Texas, there is a Franchise Tax to consider. States like Delaware and Nevada are popular for their business-friendly regulations and tax advantages. Visit your state's Secretary of State website or business filing office for detailed guidance, downloadable forms, and contact information. These sites typically offer online filing services and comprehensive FAQs to assist you in maintaining compliance with state laws.

C. Frequently Asked Questions (FAQ)

Q: What is the difference between an LLC and a corporation?

An LLC offers flexibility in management and tax options, along with personal liability protection for its members. A corporation, while also providing liability protection, has a more rigid structure and is subject to double taxation unless it qualifies as an S-corporation.

Q: Do I need an Operating Agreement for my LLC?

While not all states require an Operating Agreement, having one is highly recommended as it outlines the management structure and operating procedures, reducing the risk of disputes among members.

Q: How are LLCs taxed?

By default, single-member LLCs are taxed as sole proprietorships, and multi-member LLCs are taxed as partnerships. However, LLCs can elect to be taxed as a corporation if that structure is more beneficial.

Q: Can I convert my existing business into an LLC?

Yes, many sole proprietorships and partnerships convert to LLCs for the added liability protection and tax benefits. The process involves filing the necessary formation documents with your state and notifying the IRS of the change in business structure.

Q: What is a registered agent, and do I need one?

A registered agent is a person or entity designated to receive legal and official documents on behalf of your LLC. All LLCs are required to have a registered agent in the state where they are formed.

Q: How do I dissolve my LLC?

Dissolving an LLC involves filing dissolution documents with your state and settling all debts and obligations. This process also includes distributing any remaining assets to the members according to the terms of the Operating Agreement.

As we come to the end of this guide, it's essential to reflect on the journey of understanding and forming an LLC. We've explored what an LLC is, its advantages and disadvantages, and how it compares to other business structures. We've walked through the planning stages, covering everything from defining your business goals to choosing a registered agent and drafting an Operating Agreement. The formation process was detailed step-by-step, and we discussed the ongoing responsibilities of managing, financing, and ensuring legal compliance for your LLC.

Recap of Key Points

Throughout this guide, the critical takeaways have been the importance of thorough planning, diligent compliance with legal requirements, and proactive management of finances and operations. Understanding the nuances of LLC taxes, the significance of an Operating Agreement, and the benefits of professional services can greatly impact your business's success. Templates and checklists are invaluable tools to keep your business organized and on track. Additionally, seeking out reliable resources and continuing your education through books, courses, and professional advice is crucial for sustained growth and adaptation.

Encouragement and Next Steps

Starting and managing an LLC can be both exciting and challenging. Remember, each step you take brings you closer to realizing your entrepreneurial dreams. Don't be daunted by the complexities; instead, view them as opportunities to learn and grow. The knowledge and tools provided in this guide are just the beginning. Keep pushing forward, stay informed, and don't hesitate to seek help when needed. Your dedication and hard work will pave the way for your LLC's success. Now, equipped with this guide, take the next step confidently and start building the business you envision. The future of your LLC is in your hands, and the possibilities are endless.

www.ingramcontent.com/pod-product-compliance
Lightning Source LLC
Chambersburg PA
CBHW071213210326
41597CB00016B/1800